The small prison cell was cold and damp. He didn't have his Bible. He didn't even have a coat, and winter was coming.

A guard managed to bring him a pen and a few sheets of writing material. At last he could send a letter to those young men he had left in positions of leadership.

He wished he could have spent more time with them. He'd wanted to tell them more about how to lead a church, how to solve differences within the church family, how to spot and deal with false teachers, how to be sure of one's relationship with Christ, how to teach.

But now there was just a little time and a few scraps of paper. What could he say that would help them the most? . . .

The new generations who received those letters from the aging Paul, Peter, Jude, and John were only the first of a long line. We stand in the same line of believers who have profited from these letters. What is this treasure we have received? . . . and how shall we, too, PASS IT ON?

Other BIBLE ALIVE titles:
OLD TESTAMENT SURVEYS
Let Day Begin
Freedom Road
Years of Darkness, Days of Glory
Edge of Judgment
Springtime Coming
Lift High the Torch
NEW TESTAMENT SURVEYS
The Servant King
The Great Adventure
Regions Beyond
Christ Preeminent
His Glory

LARRY RICHARDS
BIBLE ALIVE SERIES

Pass It On

Our Heritage from the Apostolic Age
Studies in 1 and 2 Timothy, Titus, 1 and 2 Peter
Jude, 1, 2, and 3 John

G. Allen Fleece Library
Columbia International University
Columbia, SC 29203

David C. Cook Publishing Co.
ELGIN, ILLINOIS—WESTON, ONTARIO
FULLERTON, CALIFORNIA

PASS IT ON
© 1978 David C. Cook Publishing Co.

All rights reserved. With the exception of specifically indicated material and brief excerpts for review purposes, no part of this book may be reproduced or used in any form without written permission from the publisher.

Scripture quotations, unless otherwise noted, are from the New International Version.

Published by David C. Cook Publishing Co., 850 N. Grove Ave., Elgin, IL 60120
Edited by Sharrel Keyes
Cover photograph by Ed Elsner
Printed in the United States of America
ISBN 0-89191-090-5

LC 77-87260

CONTENTS

PART 1: LEADERSHIP *1, 2 Timothy; Titus*
1 Last Words 9
2 To Teach Others 20
3 Reliable Men 30
4 The Undershepherds 41

PART 2: WARNINGS *2 Peter; Jude*
5 Times of Stress 55
6 Heresy! 66

PART 3: A LIFE OF LOVE *1, 2, 3 John*
7 The Disciple Jesus Loved 81
8 To Know Him 93
9 Called to Love 104
10 Eternal Life 115

PART 4: THEOLOGY REVIEW
11 God's Personal Touch 127
12 God Stoops to Care 137
13 God and His Family 148

LEADER SUPPLEMENT 161

Part One
LEADERSHIP
1 and 2 Timothy; Titus

1
1, 2 Timothy; Titus

LAST WORDS

I LIKE TO READ the last words of famous men, even when I suspect someone else may have put those words in the celebrity's mouth. Examples of questionable but famous last words include those of the Emperor Julian, vigorous opponent of Christianity in the A.D. 360's, who supposedly said, "Thou has conquered, O pale Galilean." And there was the millionaire whose last words to his gathered sons was reported to be "Remember . . . buy low and sell high."

But last words do give us insight into the values, concerns, and focus of a life. They also lead me to wonder, what advice do I want to pass on to my children? If I could record not just a saying but a solid core of guidance for future generations, what would I say?

Pretentious! Yes, it would be pretentious for you or me to presume to look ahead and give words of wisdom to guide future generations of our families.

BIBLE ALIVE SERIES

We're so limited in our understanding that we can't see what the next year holds, much less decades. But as we come to Paul's final letters in the New Testament, and to other late writings, we recognize the fact that we are reading last words that are applicable to us today. These letters are guidelines for living as God's family in a world that is all too often an enemy of Christian values.

These letters are not only the wisdom of men long experienced as Christian leaders, but words written under the inspiration of the Holy Spirit.

The first thirty years of the New Testament era have passed now. Jesus has entered history. The church has developed after His death and resurrection. The power of the gospel has brought hope and new life to millions of first-century pagans. The church has responded to opposition and attack by affirming Christ as the center of its life and by understanding itself as His Body, His Family, His Holy Temple. The men and women who were the driving force the early years . . . Paul, Peter, Barnabas, John, Apollos, Priscilla, all the others . . . are now old.

There have been other changes. Christianity is no longer a novelty. The church knows second- and even third-generation believers. Once each Christian was a convert from paganism or Judaism, but now young men and women have grown up knowing the truths of the faith. Soon the Roman government will take an official position against Christianity. Within the faith, false teachers intrude, infiltrating twisted doctrine and warped life-styles.

A clear form of organization with definite offices

and roles has developed within the church. How that organization is to function, without taking on the unhealthy characteristics of bureaucracy, is another challenge the church has to face.

During the decades of the sixties through the nineties, Paul and the others looked ahead to the emerging problems and needs. They also knew that they must commit their ministry to others who would faithfully carry on the work of God. Thus they were led to leave us, in 1 and 2 Timothy and Titus, in Jude and 2 Peter, and in the three letters of John, their last words. These letters speak to us today with a living authority that is part of our heritage from the apostolic age.

PAUL, TIMOTHY, AND TITUS

Paul. The Book of Acts closes with Paul imprisoned in Rome. Most commentators feel that he arrived there (Acts 28) about A.D. 59. Kept under very lenient restraint, he had his own rented home and many visitors. It was during this time that he wrote the Prison Epistles of Colossians, Ephesians, Philippians, and Philemon. The apostle eventually gained the opportunity to appeal to the emperor and was released.

Paul then very probably made his intended visit to Spain. An early church father, Clement of Rome, reports that Paul went to "the extreme limit of the west" before suffering martyrdom. We can gather that he also had time to visit Ephesus and Macedonia (1 Tim. 1:3) as well as Crete (Titus 1:5). He planned to spend the winter in Nicopolis on the west coast of Epirus (Tit. 3:12). Certainly the apostle was again free, totally immersed in his ministries of missionary and church supervisor.

But when Paul writes 2 Timothy, he is imprisoned a second time, and this time under no gentle restraint: he is in chains (2 Tim. 1:16) and lacks both warm clothing and books (2 Tim. 4:13). The prospect is so grim that Paul writes, "I am already being poured out as a drink offering, and the time has come for my departure" (2 Tim. 4:6).

What has happened?

Paul's release from his first imprisonment probably took place around A.D. 60 or 61. His journey to Spain may have taken two years, say till 63. On his return he revisited many churches and wrote supportive letters to young Timothy and Titus (late 63, early 64). Then came a series of events that unleashed opposition to Christianity throughout the empire.

Nero Claudius Caesar was emperor of Rome from A.D. 54 to 67. Although a vicious and unbalanced man, his first five years were marked by sound administration because he was content to let two supporters, Seneca and Burrus, run the empire. By 62, however, the young emperor grasped the full power of his position, having put to death those who had previously restrained him (including his mother). The situation rapidly deteriorated. In July of 64 a fire broke out in a slum and destroyed half of Rome, and the rumor circulated that Nero had put his capital to the torch in order to have more space for one of his grandiose building schemes.

The increasingly unpopular emperor looked for a scapegoat upon whom he could turn the wrath of the people. Christians, already hated by the Roman mob, were chosen. During the next five years suppression of Christianity became the official policy of the Roman state, and persecution was intensified.

Paul was rearrested, tumbled into a maximum security prison in Rome, and, within months after writing his second letter to Timothy, was executed. Deserted and alone during his last days (see 2 Tim. 4: 16), the aged apostle's final thoughts were for the harassed church and the youthful leaders who must now accept the burden of guiding its course.

Timothy. Our impressions of Timothy come from Acts and the letters he received from Paul. Timothy was a youth of good reputation, probably a resident of Lystra (Acts 16: 2). His father was a Greek and his mother a devout Jewess who, with his grandmother Lois, instructed Timothy in the Old Testament Scriptures (Acts 16: 1; 2 Tim. 1: 5, 14). Timothy was probably a teen when he first joined Paul; fifteen years later Paul would write, "Don't let anyone look down on you because you are young" (1 Tim. 4: 12).

It's uncertain how heavily Timothy was involved in missionary work during the intervening years; however, his name keeps appearing in association with Paul or Silas. Certainly Paul had known this young man intimately. He now commits to him much of his own ministry and gives his last words of advice. Certainly, Paul is aware not only of the difficulties facing the church but of Timothy's own weaknesses. Bastien Van Elderen, New Testament scholar and archaeologist, sums up the impression of Timothy conveyed in Paul's writings:

"He was a fairly young man who was somewhat retiring, perhaps even a bit shy. He appears to be sincere and devoted, but at times perhaps frightened by his opponents and their teachings. This perhaps is also reflected in his apparent inability to cope with the problems in the Corinthian church."

How encouraging it is to see the mission of the church being committed to ordinary people. Retiring. Perhaps shy. Sincere, but uncomfortable with opposition, and all too often unable to cope. Just ordinary people like you and me. Yet Christ's church has endured and from generation to generation communicated the life that is the Savior's enduring gift to those who choose to make Him their own. How important then Paul's last words to Timothy will be. They will comfort us ordinary people and give us guidelines for maintaining the Church of Jesus Christ as His living, growing family.

Titus. We know even less of Titus than of Timothy, yet the infrequent reference in the Epistles to this young leader is consistently favorable. He shows genuine devotion and concern (2 Cor. 8:16-17); he is committed to those he serves (12:18). And Titus was apparently effective even in areas in which Timothy proved indecisive. Van Elderen reflects on the impact of Titus's visit to Corinth as Paul's emissary during a time of antagonism against the aging apostle.

When Paul arrived in Troas, he did not find Titus (2 Cor. 1:13). Although there were promising opportunities for mission work in Troas, Paul's concern about Corinth and Titus led him to proceed to Macedonia.... In Macedonia Titus brings to Paul a comforting report about the Corinthians, which gives him much joy and peace of mind (2 Cor. 7:6-14). Titus seems to have established a good rapport with the Corinthians and Paul exuberantly expresses his gratitude for the happy turn of events.[1]

Aside from this portrait of an effective and promising young leader, we know only that Titus was a Gentile who remained uncircumcised. He, like Timothy, accompanied Paul and later Barnabas on missionary journeys. Now, like Timothy, Titus must provide leadership in place of the apostle, and like Timothy, he would profit from Paul's final advice.

ISSUES AND ANSWERS

The emphasis of each of these three letters is different. We might suggest that in 1 Timothy Paul's focus is the life to which the church is called. In 2 Timothy Paul's focus is the work to which leaders are committed. The letter to Titus, on the other hand, emphasizes the way in which the church is to accomplish God's purposes in this world.

Yet despite different emphases, there is constant overlap of content and recurring themes that find parallel expression in each. The chart on pages 16-17 shows areas of overlap and helps us see how certain critical issues grasped the apostle's attention

ISSUE AND ANSWERS
Common Content in the Pastoral Epistles

THE LIFE OF THE CHURCH 1 Timothy	THE WORK OF LEADERS 2 Timothy	THE WAY OF THE BODY Titus
1:3-7 Goal of ministry: love from pure heart	1:3-12 Called to holy life, fervent love	1:1-4 Concern for "knowledge of the truth that leads to godliness"
1:8-11 Life-style contrary to *sound doctrine* described	1:13-14 Must guard *sound doctrine*	
1:12-17 Paul an example of a saved sinner; "eternal" life	1:15-18 Onesiphorus an example	
1:18-20 Timothy's goal to be a minister of the faith	2:1-7 Timothy to entrust truth to faithful men who will minister	
2:1-7 Pray and live to bring salvation to others	2:8-13 Paul's endurance for the salvation of elect	
2:8-9 Examples of godly life	2:14-19 Leaders must live godly lives	
2:11-15 Special limits placed on women's role	2:20-21 Limits placed by individual's response	
3:1-15 Leaders' qualifications	2:22-26 How a leader lives, teaches, and corrects	1:5-9 Leader's example 1:10-16 Leader's duties

4:1-5	False life-style	3:1-9	False leaders
4:6-10	Danger of distraction from godliness		
4:11-16	Need to set example in faith, speech, life, etc.	3:10-17	Need to continue in godly life and teaching
5:1-8	Respect toward others in the family: "put religion into practice"	4:1-5	Need to preach and live true doctrine
5:9-16	Widows' role		
5:17-20	Elders' responsibility		
5:21-25	Various injunctions		
6:1-2	Slaves' attitude		
6:3-10	False doctrine; wrong motives		
6:11-21	Charge to pursue godliness, truth, love, etc., keep faith in Christ central	4:6-18	Paul an example of perservering workman, athlete

2:1-15	Godly life and doctrine applied		
3:1f	Practical results of our common salvation		

BIBLE ALIVE SERIES

in his final days. We can best understand the teaching of these last letters not by studying each separately but by examining them together, looking for Paul's answers to common and recurring issues.

What a heritage these letters are. Christ's Church was designed to endure. Though at times its grasp of spiritual realities has seemed weak and its life flame dimmed, the Church has endured. Yet enduring is not God's sole goal for His family. God yearns for us to live fully. The gift of His life is ours in Christ: the great desire of God's heart for us is that we might experience that life to the full.

Our problem of how to experience real, vital life in an enduring institution, the ongoing, structured church, has been answered in the providence and purpose of God. The answer is one we will come to understand and experience to an even fuller degree as we meet ourselves in the issues raised by Paul and the others.

GOING DEEPER

Suggestions to guide and stimulate your personal study of the Bible text.

to personalize
1. Looking at the world situation and your own family today, what last words would you like to leave your children or loved ones? What values would you be particularly concerned that they hold and apply?
2. Read quickly through these three letters. What thought seems most important to you personally?

to probe

1. Read carefully through the three letters, looking especially for words or themes that recur. Make a list of your observations.
2. Select two parallel sections from the chart on pages 16-17. How are the paragraphs in each letter similar? Different? What underlying issue seems to be the focus of Paul's concern?

1. Merrill Tenney, ed. *Zondervan Pictorial Bible Dictionary,* 5 vols. (Grand Rapids: Zondervan, 1975), 5:759.

2
1, 2 Timothy; Titus

TO TEACH OTHERS

OVER AND OVER AGAIN in Paul's last words to Timothy and Titus, he returns to the theme of teaching. His concern seems obvious. Certainly the continuation of the Church across the ages demands transmission of Bible truths. Probably one of the most quoted verses from the pastoral Epistles is 2 Timothy 2:2: "And the things you have heard me say in the presence of many witnesses entrust to reliable men who will also be qualified to teach others."

This verse appears on the seal of the seminary I attended. It's a common theme at seminary commencements. Much of our education in Sunday school as well as in special training and discipleship classes hopes to do just this: entrust the task of teaching so that truth may be passed on to the next generation.

But we're so confident we know what "teaching" means that we may fail to ask what it meant to Paul when he wrote to young Timothy and Titus.

EDUCATION

The Random House Dictionary defines *education* as "the act or process of imparting or acquiring general knowledge, developing the powers of reasoning and judgment, and generally of preparing oneself or others intellectually for mature life." In our society *education* implies *school,* and to us the key phrases in this dictionary definition are "imparting or acquiring knowledge" and "preparing oneself intellectually." To teach or to learn, to be educated, focuses on knowledge and the intellect.

This is, of course, an accurate definition for our society. School systems teach reading and writing, history and science, business and law, so learners will be "prepared intellectually for mature life." In our society teaching is imparting knowledge and processing information; learning is acquiring knowledge and using information. It's hard for us to realize that teaching did not have the same meaning for Paul or Timothy or other early readers of these letters.

William Barclay, in *Educational Ideals in the Ancient World,* suggests that Jewish education was very different from our notions of teaching and learning.

> The very basis of Judaism is to be found in the conception of holiness. 'Ye shall be holy for I the Lord your God am holy.' 'And ye shall be holy unto me: for I the Lord am holy, and have severed you from other people that ye might be mine.' That is to say, *it was the*

destiny of the Jewish people to be different. Holiness means difference. And their whole educational system was directed to that end. It has been precisely that educational system which has kept the Jewish race in existence. The Jew is no longer a racial type; he is a person who follows a certain way of life, and who belongs to a certain faith. If Jewish religion had faltered, or altered, the Jews would have ceased to exist. First and foremost, the Jewish ideal of education is the ideal of holiness, of difference, of separation from all other peoples in order to belong to God. Their educational system was nothing less than the instrument by which their existence as a nation, and their fulfillment of their destiny, was ensured.[1]

See what Barclay is saying? The Hebrew concept of education was not to impart knowledge or prepare oneself intellectually, but to produce holiness and to communicate a distinctive life-style. When Paul wrote to Timothy and Titus about the importance of teaching in the church, his concept of education was Hebrew, not twentieth-century.

What does this mean for us? First, it illustrates why we must guard against reading a twentieth-century meaning into Bible words. Secondly, it encourages us to explore Scripture in order to determine from the Bible itself the meaning of such terms as *teach* and *instruct*.

We need to carefully examine these letters to find out what kind of teaching and learning Paul was so concerned about. Do we have his kind of teaching in our churches today? Are there better ways to communicate our faith to coming generations than we have found? How do we pass on our living relationship with Jesus Christ to others?

GOALS OF EDUCATION

In each of his three last letters Paul seems to plunge immediately into statements about the goal of Christian teaching. In 1 Timothy he warns against false doctrine and urges commitment to the truth. He states succinctly his goal of teaching the truth: "love which comes from a pure heart, a good conscience and a sincere faith" (1 Tim. 1:5). In 2 Timothy he brings up the same issue: "What you have heard from me, keep as the pattern of sound teaching, with faith and love in Christ Jesus (1:13). And in the opening of Titus, Paul speaks immediately of "the knowledge of the truth that leads to godliness" (1:1). The goals Paul has in mind for teaching in the church are not limited to gaining intellectual knowledge. In fact, Bible knowledge is never an end in itself but is to produce love, faith, and godliness.

Measuring learning. Paul was not so much concerned that believers *knew* the truth as he was that the truth produced in them a distinctive way of life. The measure of effective teaching is not how much the learner knows, but the *quality* of his life.

Schools evaluate learning by testing and measuring knowledge. How many books has the student read? What were his final grades? Were the answers on the exam correct? Within the church, there's a tendency to think of the educated Christian as someone who has gone to Bible school, a Christian college, or seminary. The individual who has memorized the most Bible verses, who always has the right answer to a doctrinal question, or who can authoritatively chart a premillennial picture of the future may be viewed as the model of a well-taught Christian.

But if we take our stance with the apostle Paul, we realize that evidence of Christian learning is not found in what is known but in the love, faith, and godliness that mark the believer's life. Paul urges Timothy and Titus to be engaged in the kind of teaching that links truth with life; the kind of teaching that has as its product loving, trusting, and godly men and women. Paul would say that character is a better indicator of a well-taught Christian than knowledge!

TRUTH . . . AND LIFE

One of my old friends, a coprofessor at a school where I taught, is a dichotomous thinker. That is, he tends to think in opposites in either/or fashion. At one time the faculty senate began to talk of redesigning our curriculum to better equip young people for the practical demands of the ministry. My friend became visibly upset. If our curriculum were to be "practical," we would have to sacrifice "academic respectability." Education must be either "academic" (concentrating on truth) or "practical" (concentrating on methodology), and *he* was going to stand firmly on the side of truth! He could never see education involving *both* the academic *and* the practical. For him it must be either one or the other.

But nothing could be further from the apostle Paul's thought in these letters. To him, teaching's goal is knowledge expressed in love, faith, and godliness; truth and life must be intimately linked.

- Paul says sinful acts are "contrary to sound doctrine" and do not conform to the "glorious gospel of the blessed God" (1 Tim. 1: 9-11).
- Paul expresses concern about "how people ought to conduct themselves in God's household, which is the church of the living God, the pillar and foundation of the truth" (1 Tim. 3: 15).
- Paul's goal is "knowledge of the truth that leads to godliness" (Titus 1: 1).
- Paul teaches that temperance, self-control, faith, love, endurance, and reverence are "in accord with sound doctrine" (Titus 2: 1-3).
- Paul encourages Titus to stress basic doctrinal truths "so that those who have trusted in God may be careful to devote themselves to doing what is good" (Titus 3: 8).

Looking over these statements, we can see several things. 1) Knowing the truth, being committed to sound doctrine, must lead to godliness, love, self-control, reverence, etc. 2) Not only is truth expected to have an impact on life, but life is to be in harmony with truth. Our good works will reflect our beliefs. 3) Truth produces the godly life-style, not vice versa. Being a "good person" does not bring one to the truth. But truth, accepted and applied, does produce goodness in us.

The kind of teaching that Paul urges links truth and life and communicates both content and lifestyle. Teaching that attempts to communicate the faith simply as a good way of life is woefully inadequate; but teaching that attempts to communicate the faith merely as a system of beliefs is just as wrong!

Our twentieth-century emphasis on teaching as the transmission of information is *not* an adequate model for teaching God's Word.

What, then, is this teaching that Paul so urgently demands?

TEACHING

In Paul's first letter to Timothy, he gives him quite a list of subjects to teach, including: exposure of false doctrines, myths and genealogies; law; sound doctrine; the glorious gospel; mercy, truth, dedication, prayer; harmony; women's dress and appearance; marriage and dietary practices; qualifications for leaders; conduct; sayings, truths of the faith; the practice of religion, relationships with fellow Christians, treatment of widows; ways to select elders; contentment, righteousness, faith, love, endurance, hope in God, and doing good.

In looking over even this incomplete list, someone may argue, "But this isn't about teaching." That argument, of course, presupposes the narrow idea that teaching involves only concepts and beliefs, communicated by lectures or dramatizations.

But that is the whole point. Paul was concerned with communicating doctrine, mercy, commitment, conduct—all of life. *Christian communication touches the entire person:* beliefs, attitudes, values, behaviors.

To teach the whole person, instruction must go far beyond information processing. If we return to 1 Timothy, we will see that biblical teaching involves verbal instruction, yes. But it also involves urging, pointing out, commanding, setting examples, expressing desires, preaching, charging, giving instructions: involvement and activity significantly touching every point of the learner's life. One of the first and most significant truths we grasp in the Pastorals is that we must help individuals bring their whole lives into harmony with God.

If we study the Pastorals carefully, we discover that Paul's stress on instruction focuses more often on life-style than on truth. These second-generation Christians knew and accepted doctrinal truths. What they needed most was to live their lives in harmony with the truth they knew. We might summarize Paul's concept of teaching by using his own words: "helping the people of God learn how to conduct themselves in God's household" (1 Tim. 3:15). And the goal of this New Testament kind of teaching? To produce love (1 Tim. 1:5)!

ON GUARD

Paul's emphasis on teaching is meant to help the early church, and you and me today, avoid tragic

BIBLE ALIVE SERIES

errors. On the one hand, believers cannot neglect doctrine if we are to know reality. On the other hand, if believers think only orthodox doctrine is important, we can end up with debates, hatred between true believers, and, finally, sterility of life.

We can take pride in our rightness, cutting ourselves off from others who differ from us. Yet with all our knowledge, we can fail to experience the warmth and vitality of a growing relationship with God and with our brothers and sisters in Christ.

The kind of teaching that stresses *only* knowledge is all too likely to produce this sterile experience. When we teach our children by stressing mastery of stories, information, and doctrines, we are likely to produce young people who have the right answers, but who do not know the living touch of Jesus. Paul urges us to guard against this pitfall by communicating the full gospel: faith is both truth and life-style.

In our next two studies we'll see how the full gospel should be taught. We'll see the importance of spiritual leaders in the church, and how leaders can communicate Christ's life along with true doctrine. For now it's important that we understand how the apostle Paul defines teaching and learning.

GOING DEEPER

to personalize

1. In order to see for yourself the emphasis on teaching in Paul's letters, do one of the following:
- From 2 Timothy, list everything Paul wants taught. In a second list, find all the ways he tells

Timothy to communicate this full gospel.

● Study carefully Titus 2. In this brief section of fifteen verses, the word *teach* is used seven times. Examine these verses carefully, and write out Paul's definition of teaching. Be ready to explain your definition in class.

2. Think back on your own Christian education. What kind of teaching have you had? What have you learned? What do you think are the strengths and weaknesses of your experience? How might you improve on it?

3. Imagine that you have been given the task of designing a Christian education program for your own church for eighth-graders. What kind of teaching program do you feel Paul might approve of? What would you want to avoid?

to probe

1. What concepts of teaching can you find in Acts, or any other New Testament book?

2. Evaluate the teaching ministry of a local church other than your own. Talk with leaders and members. What is their concept of teaching? Can they define the sound doctrine Christians believe? Can they define the godly life-style Christians are to live?

---

1. William Barclay, *Educational Ideals in the Ancient World* (Grand Rapids, Baker Book House, 1974), p. 47.

3
1, 2 Timothy; Titus

RELIABLE MEN

NOT LONG AGO the headlines carried news of two *747s* that collided on the ground in a fog, killing hundreds. The verdict of the investigators? "Human error." The safety system was foolproof, but one of the pilots had not correctly followed procedures.

As I write this, a great debate goes on about the use of nuclear power to supplement power generated by coal and oil. "Unsafe!" cry the environmentalists. "Foolproof," respond the electric companies. Yet there is the nagging doubt that no matter how foolproof the system, there may be room for human error.

Our systems may be perfect, but people are not. We must always consider the human element.

A communication system. In the last chapter we saw Paul's deep concern for effective communication of the faith to succeeding generations. Sound doctrine and the distinctive Christian way of life must be taught. The pastoral Epistles describe a system of teaching designed to transmit both truth and life.

Dr. Merrill Tenney has pointed out that topics touched on in Titus alone constitute a fair digest of New Testament theology, and goes on to list the following:

- The personality of God (2:11; 3:6)
- The qualities of His love and grace (2:11; 3:4)
- His title of Saviour (2:10; 3:4)
- The saviourhood of Christ (2:13; 3:6)
- The Holy Spirit (3:5)
- The implication of the triune being of God (3:5-6)
- The essential deity of Christ (2:13)
- The vicarious atonement of Christ (2:14)
- The universality of salvation (2:11)
- Salvation by grace, not works (3:5)
- The incoming of the Holy Spirit (3:5)
- Justification by faith (3:7)
- Sanctification (purification) of his own people (2:14)
- Separation from evil (2:12)
- Inheritance of eternal life (3:7)
- The return of Christ (2:13)[1]

These truths are to be affirmed and maintained.

But if we read Titus again, we find that this brief book also gives a fair summary of Christian lifestyle! Here we read about: godliness (1:1), faith (1:2; 2:2), qualities of leaders (1:5-9), ministry of leaders (1:8-9), temperance (2:2), love (2:2, 4), self-control (2:2, 5-6, 12), endurance (2:2), dedication to good (2:7; 3:1, 8, 14), personal integrity (2:7, 10), seriousness (2:7), subjection to authority

(2:9; 3:1), trustworthiness (2:10), rejection of sin (2:12), humility (3:2), considerateness (3:2), peaceableness (3:2), and harmony (3:10). This doctrine, and this way of life, Paul yearns to pass on to the next generation through the system of teaching and communication that the Pastorals describe.

Yet the apostle is deeply aware that no system is foolproof; we must pay the closest attention to the human element. So over and over Paul focuses our attention on the "reliable men" (2 Tim. 2:2) to whom the faith is to be entrusted: men who will be able "to teach others."

THEIR SELECTION

In both 1 Timothy and Titus Paul describes the qualifications and responsibilities of church leaders.
- They are to manage (take care of) the church (1 Tim. 3:5).
- They are to be entrusted with God's work (Titus 1:7).
- They are to both encourage and refute with sound doctrine (Titus 1:9).

In essence, leaders are to be responsible for both the beliefs and the life-style of the local Christian community. Whether they are called pastors or elders or deacons, they are the communicators of the faith.

What sounds foreign to us about Paul's guidelines for selecting leaders is that he does not stress academic or intellectual equipment. True, the leader must "keep hold of the deep truths of the faith with a clear conscience" (1 Tim. 3:9) and "hold firmly to the trustworthy message as it has been taught" (Titus 1:9). But apart from this commitment to sound doctrine, and a grasp of truth that enables the leader to encourage, rebuke, and explain (2 Tim. 4:2), little is said about knowledge. What the apostle does stress is character, or quality of life. The person recognized as a leader and given responsibility for teaching in the church is to be above reproach, married to but one wife, temperate, self-controlled, respectable and upright, hospitable, not an alcoholic, not violent but gentle, not quarrelsome or quick-tempered, not a money lover, a good manager of his family, not a recent convert (who might be susceptible to conceit), well respected by non-Christians, not overbearing, a lover of good, holy, and disciplined. Qualities such as these, rather than verbal ability or success in business or the capacity to preach a good sermon, are to be given first consideration in selecting leaders in a local church.

We ask, "Why?" Why not give first consideration to a seminary transcript, or capacity to preach, or previous success, or talent, or spiritual giftedness? Yet on such qualifications Paul remains strangely silent.

"Paul, what spiritual gifts should a leader have?" No answer.

"Paul, what kind of training should a leader have?" Silence.

"Paul, should we choose a successful businessman or well-known community leader?" Only silence.

"But Paul, isn't it important for the leader to be

able to preach an interesting sermon?" Again, except for his remark that a leader should be adept at teaching, there is no response. Instead, Paul points us away from such considerations and says over and over again, look first to the *quality* of the life.

But *why?* Because leaders are to *live* God's truth.

If teaching in the church involved only *knowing*, then those whose knowledge was superior should be leaders. But for Christians, truth and life are both vital. Using biblical knowledge to form sound doctrine means knowing by experience: it leads invariably to the distinctive life-style Paul highlights in these letters. The goal of teaching sound doctrine is to produce love (1 Tim. 1:5) and godliness (Titus 1:1).

Isn't it obvious, then, that we should choose leaders who are approaching that goal, rather than those who may simply be starting on the way? Isn't it clear that conceptual, schooled knowledge of the Bible may be a step toward understanding Christian truth, but it is not the goal itself? Anyone who is short of the goal, who relies on his or her intellectual knowledge alone, should never be considered for spiritual leadership.

This is the underlying reason for Paul's repeating his list of qualifications for leadership in the church. The person recognized as a teacher in the community of faith must have already *learned*. We recognize such a person by character, not transcripts.

HOW LEADERS TEACH

So far we've seen that teaching in the biblical sense is

not teaching in our sense of education. For the distinctive task of transmitting both true doctrine and vital life-style, rather than just knowledge for its own sake, we are to choose leaders whose qualifications are demonstrated by their devotion. Those who are spiritual will be able to guide and teach the church, while the unspiritual, no matter how much they know, will not be able to maintain or build God's family.

These final letters of Paul are full of insights into *how* leaders can build and maintain the church family.

How Paul taught Timothy. We can only understand Paul's discipling of Timothy if we remember that they spent the better part of fifteen years together. Young Timothy shared Paul's life, listening to the great apostle as he taught, watching as Paul responded to persecution and to adulation, sharing moments of stress, joys, and defeats. No wonder Paul could remind him now, "You, however, know all about my teaching, my way of life, my purpose, faith, patience, love, endurance, persecutions, sufferings" (2 Tim. 3:10). Paul's beliefs, his character, his actions—public and private—were a model for Timothy. "What you have heard from me," Paul wrote, "Keep as the pattern of sound teaching, with faith and love in Christ Jesus" (2 Tim. 1:13). Paul explained doctrine and he demonstrated a godly life.

How Timothy is to teach. "Pursue righteousness, faith, love and peace," Paul urges (2 Tim. 2:22). "Continue in what you have learned and have become convinced of" (3:14). Timothy is not only to command and teach truth; he is to "set an example for the believers in speech, in life, in love, in faith and purity" (1 Tim. 4:12). He is to give himself wholly to his ministry and to "watch your life and doctrine closely" (1 Tim. 4:16), "so that everyone may see your progress" (1 Tim. 4:12). The process of communication does involve instruction, but it also requires that the teacher be willing to live out the teaching. The person whose own life expresses the faith is essential in God's plan for Christian teaching.

The elements of Christian life-style and the qualifications for Christian leaders show some interesting correlations.

Christian life-style includes	*Christian leaders are*
• godliness	• above reproach
• faith	• temperate
• temperance	• self-controlled
• love	• respectable and upright
• self-control	
• endurance	• hospitable
• dedication to good	• not alcoholics
• integrity	• not violent but gentle
• seriousness	• not quarrelsome or quick-tempered
• subjection to authority	
• trustworthiness	• not money lovers
• humility	• well-respected by nonbelievers
• considerateness	
• peaceableness	• lovers of good

Looking at the two side by side makes it clear. It takes a person like the one described on the right to teach the way of life described on the left. Think how foolish it would be to expect a violent or competitive person to help others become peaceable and humble. How foolish it would be to ask a money-hungry or morally loose person to teach godliness to others. How impossible to ask an intemperate or impulsive person to guide others into a life of self-control and integrity.

Ability to communicate ideas may not depend on character; a dissolute individual may express information brilliantly. But only a person who *lives* the Christian life can lead others into the life-style that truth produces.

The Bible's approach to teaching by word and example suggests several implications. The first is that the classroom or lecture hall, in which individuals gather infrequently for impersonal contact with an instructor, is inadequate for the total communication the Bible portrays. Somehow the learner needs to see the teacher in real life, if life-style is to be caught.

A second implication grows immediately from the first. It's important that a personal relationship between the Christian leader and the learner be developed. How can we learn faith, patience, temperance, love, and self-control from a stranger? We need a Paul/Timothy closeness that enables us to say, "You know all about my teaching, my way of life, my purpose, faith, patience, love, endurance, persecutions, sufferings" (2 Tim. 3:10). We can know these things only if leader and learner are close, sharing friends.

Each of these considerations implies a kind of fellowship and closeness that is uniquely a part of the Body of Christ. As we come to know and love one another, we have opportunity to learn from each other and especially from leaders to whom God has entrusted the health of the church and the communication of the faith.

LEADERS ALONE?

Scripture teaches that leaders bear the responsibility for the community: they are entrusted with the task of building and maintaining both soundness of doctrine and depth of Christian experience. In this context they are portrayed as the overseers and managers of the local congregation. Peter exhorts those recognized as leaders (elders) to "be shepherds of God's flock that is under your care, serving as overseers . . . not lording it over those entrusted to you, but being examples to the flock" (1 Pet. 5:2-3).

But is this kind of communication the sole preserve of leaders? Or is this open to all of us? The Bible says each of us is to communicate our faith in exactly the same way, by Word and life!

In the Old Testament we find Scripture's command for parents to communicate the reality of God: "These words which I command you this day shall be upon your heart; and you shall teach them diligently to your children, and shall talk of them when you sit in your house, and when you walk by the way, and when you lie down, and when you rise"

(Deut. 6:6-8). The teacher is qualified by having the "word in the heart," having an intimate relationship, and being a daily example, observable and available for sharing. We who are parents communicate our faith by instruction and example as God helps us reach our heart's desire, bringing up our children in the Lord.

It's the same in communicating our faith to unbelievers. Peter encourages us to "always be prepared to give an answer to everyone who asks you to give the reason for the hope you have," speaking "with gentleness and respect" (1 Pet. 3:15-16). In the context it is clear that Peter expects the Christian's unusual way of life to be observed and to raise questions. Example leads to explanation, and together the spoken Word and demonstrated life portray to those outside the faith the reality of Jesus Christ.

It's clear, then, that the system of communicating Christian faith described by Paul is *not* limited to leaders alone. Whoever wants to share Jesus' love has the powerful and inseparable resources of Word and example to teach others of Him.

GOING DEEPER

to personalize

1. Read 1 Timothy 3 and Titus. Then paraphrase the list of qualifications of elders and deacons, using a dictionary or thesaurus to pick the best synonym for each trait.

2. After paraphrasing the qualifications list, think about your own congregation. Who seems most

qualified for spiritual leadership?

3. The persons you named in (2) may or may not be presently recognized as leaders in your church. How are leaders selected in your congregation? Do you see any relationship between the selection process and your own leader candidates?

4. If you have a family, select one doctrine and one life-style quality you want to communicate to your children. Describe how you will go about sharing them.

to probe

1. Imagine that you have been given the task of writing for your church constitution the method of calling a new pastor. Base your approach on both the qualifications for leadership developed in the letters to Timothy and Titus and the nature of biblical teaching explored in chapter 2. Take the time to write up thoroughly the procedures you might adopt.

2. Gather information from several different churches, then describe the average approach to calling a pastor. Point up exactly *why* these systems are inadequate.

3. Develop a thorough approach to selecting elders (deacons, or board members) in your own church. How would you make sure that the right persons were chosen?

---

1. Merrill Tenney, *New Testament Survey* (Grand Rapids: Eerdmans, 1961), p. 338.

4
1, 2 Timothy; Titus

THE UNDERSHEPHERDS

WHEN PAUL and other early missionaries established a new church, they characteristically stayed for a time, teaching and instructing. They would make another visit to the young church at a later time to complete what was unfinished "and appoint elders in every town" (Titus 1: 5). From this practice, referred to in the Book of Acts and several New Testament Epistles, we draw both principles and some questions.

• Paul (and Timothy and Titus) did not function as local church leaders! What were they then?

• Elders (plural) were to be established in every town. Nothing is said about ordaining "a pastor" of a local church. What was the task of elders? What about pastors?

• Elders were appointed on the missionaries' *return* visit. Why not on the first visit?

BIBLE ALIVE SERIES

- New Testament letters dealing with leadership seem to assume (or to explicitly teach) male leadership. What about women in the local church? Can't they be pastors or elders?

Exploring questions like these does not necessarily lead us to challenge our own church government. But it does help us think more clearly about spiritual leadership in the church.

LEADERSHIP

Several different words identify church leaders in the New Testament.

Apostle. This word, which in the New Testament can mean "ambassador," "delegate," or "messenger" (i.e., "missionary") is used predominately of that group of church leaders who had a special position in the early church. They proclaimed the gospel and also held special authority to govern the Church as a whole. Jesus' first disciples, with Paul, are the men most often designated as apostles. Whether or not there are to be apostles today is often debated. What is important to note, however, is that the New Testament apostolic ministry extended beyond the local congregation.

Bishops. The Greek word we translate "bishop" means "overseer," or "one who takes care of." Jesus is called "bishop of your souls" (1 Pet. 2:25, KJV), a phrase the Revised Standard Version appropriately translates "Guardian." This word speaks of special responsibility to superintend. The parallel descriptions of qualifications for *bishop* (or overseer) in 1

Timothy 3 and for *elder* in Titus 1 suggest that these two terms, along with *shepherd, presbyter,* and *pastor,* are synonymous. The Titus passage especially seems to use "bishop" and "elder" interchangeably. Paul's letter to the Philippian church is addressed to three groups in the congregation: "all the saints . . . with the bishops and deacons" (Phil. 1:1).

Elder. This Greek word, like our own, refers first to age: "older one." The Romans had a similar term in Latin: *senatus,* or "senator." The Jews used *elder* as a title for members of local councils and for the inner group of the Sanhedrin.

In early Christianity, teams of elders were responsible for overseeing local congregations; their ministry included exhortation and preaching. Many denominations and groups today use this terminology, usually calling some "teaching elders" (preachers, ministers) and others "ruling elders" (lay leaders).

Deacons. The Greek word means "to serve" or "to wait on." A deacon is literally the servant of someone. The deacon in the New Testament church was a helper, or agent, of the governing authorities.

In Acts 6 the apostles appointed deacons to supervise food distribution to needy Christian widows. There were high spiritual qualifications for this service; yet it was recognized as a subordinate ministry established to free the apostles for teaching and prayer.

What is important to note is that on both the local and "national" levels there were men who accepted responsibility for maintaining sound doctrine and holy life-style for the church.

MULTIPLE LOCAL LEADERSHIP

Some see the Pastorals and other New Testament books as challenging our contemporary practice of hiring a single pastor. It's clear from 1 Timothy 5:17-18 that some local church leaders in Paul's time gave their full time to ministry and were supported by the congregation, "especially those whose work is preaching and teaching" (1 Tim. 5:17). So the problem does not seem to be whether or not local leaders should be paid professionals.

Where many of our churches are more seriously challenged by the New Testament Epistles is our typical organizational structure in which a lone pastor emerges as "the man at the top." We often see this structure as a pyramid with the pastor (or "senior pastor") at the peak and all others (associate pastors, board members, committee members, and ordinary laymen) under him.

But Paul speaks explicitly of "the elders who direct the affairs of the church" (1 Tim. 5:17; see also Titus 1:5). From these and other references it's clear that the New Testament concept of local church leadership is that of *team,* rather than individual "superstar," leadership.

Why multiple leadership? There may be several reasons. 1) No individual can expect to have *all* the spiritual gifts needed to adequately oversee the life of a congregation. We need a blend of gifts. 2) Leaders need to be close to individuals in the congregation and to be aware of doctrinal and practical needs. No one individual can develop close enough relationships with all members of a typical congregation. 3) We are all human and fallible. Team leadership permits discipline, correction, and instruction of leaders by other leaders. 4) Leaders give leadership by *example*. While an individual may be a good example of individual traits, no individual can model a functioning body. A leadership team can be an example of the loving, caring community the whole church is to become.

What can we learn about how local leaders are selected? I noted earlier that elders were appointed by the apostles or men like Timothy when they made *return* visits to churches. Why? The elders' qualifications focus on personal growth and maturity in the faith, evidenced both by life and grasp of sound doctrine. Persons need time to mature before their qualifications can be distinguished.

But who then selects them? In the New Testament, the apostles or their representatives seem to have made the official appointment. The word *appoint* is *epitithame,* which has the meaning of "ordain" or "give official recognition to" rather than "select." The selection process seems to have come as the congregation grew to trust and respond to their Christian lives, developed over time, commended them. They were *then* given official appointment to their office.

RELIABLE *MEN?*

Of all the questions raised about church leadership, one is particularly important and deeply felt these days: "Must leaders always be *men?* May women be elders? May women be pastors? If not, why not?" The discussion is often blurred by a semantic problem: what we in the twentieth century have defined as the elder role is not what Paul was talking about. Hence, is it even relevant to apply his qualifications to a job that sometimes more resembles that of a business manager?

Nevertheless, each of us, in whatever ecclesiastical arrangement we find ourselves, must face the general question of women's role in church leadership.

To respond to this issue, we first of all need to review how the New Testament affirms the equality of women with men in the Body of Christ. In a day and culture that typically counted only men, the number of conversations of both men and women were tallied by the Christians (see Acts 5:14; 8:12). Women were with the original disciples after Jesus' ascension; "they all joined together constantly in prayer" (Acts 1:14). The conversions of individual women are noted (Lydia in Acts 16:14-15; Damaris in 17:34). In other cases, Scripture records that "not a few prominent women" and "a number of prominent Greek women" believed (Acts 17:4, 12). Paul ends his letter to the Romans with a list of notes to special people in the church; a third of those are women.

There are women whom Paul calls his "fellow-workers" who "have contended at my side in the cause of the Gospel" (Phil. 4:3). Paul uses the word *fellow-worker* to describe Timothy (Rom. 16:21), Titus (2 Cor. 8:23), Demas and Luke (Philemon 24),

Priscilla (Rom. 16:3), and Euodia and Syntyche (Phil. 4:3), the last three being women.

Phoebe was a deaconess (Romans 16:2), and many commentators feel that 1 Timothy 3:11 refers not to deacons' wives but to deaconesses. In the practical, ongoing work of the church for which the deacons were responsible, there would be certain tasks clearly more suited to women (assisting another woman at baptism, for example).

In this age of the Spirit, even the gift of prophecy (which many feel includes proclamation or preaching) is for daughters as well as sons (Acts 2:18; 1 Cor. 11:5). In the church, each person is a priest, and each has spiritual gifts through which he or she can contribute to the health and ministry of the whole. It is completely out of harmony with the Bible to make artificial distinctions between men and women in the church, relegating women to a second-class position. Each woman and each man in the church is free to find fulfillment as a ministering person. "There is neither Jew nor Greek, slave nor free, male nor female, for you are all one in Christ Jesus" (Gal. 3:28).

Women leaders? Why then in the Pastorals does the same writer, Paul, "not permit a woman to teach or to have authority over a man"? (1 Tim. 2:12). Why are bishops and deacons referred to as "husbands" and "men" (1 Tim. 3:2, 8, 12; Titus 1:6) without exception?

In the whole context of Scripture (where women do prophesy!) it's clear that Paul is not suggesting a woman may not open her mouth when men are present. Church leadership is the topic of the Pastorals, and since leaders oversee the purity of the Christian community's doctrine and life-style, it seems clear that the "teaching" referred to is the kind of "teaching with authority" that Paul urges on Timothy and Titus as their ministry. It was Timothy's role to "command and teach" (1 Tim. 4:11) the things of God. Apparently Paul did not permit a woman to be ordained to such an office of responsibility.

Today? What about today? Well, there are many who would disagree with this instruction of Paul's.

• Some suppose that Paul was simply a male chauvinist. He spoke from the context of his own time and thus shared a common prejudice against women. "For our enlightened time," they suggest, "such a limit does not apply."

• Others, less eager to discount Scripture, still suggest that the restriction was peculiar to first-century culture. In that society, a woman leader would not have had the same respect as a man. In today's world, the situation has changed, so we are free to suppose that the restriction no longer applies.

• Others suggest that it is all right for women to serve on the church board "at the invitation of" (and thus under the authority of) the men of the congregation.

Among those who take Paul's restriction at face value are the following:

• Some say that his ruling is based not in culture but in creation. God ordained male headship as long ago as Genesis 2, not because of any superior intelligence or strength, but simply because headship has to be vested somewhere to prevent anarchy. In everyday society, we may rearrange roles and responsibilities to our hearts' content, but in the home and the church—divinely ordained institutions—we are bound to follow the order demonstrated in Scripture.

- Some extremists make this teaching the foundation of their attack on women as persons, declaring that the disqualifications for church leadership demonstrates female inferiority.
- Still others simply say that whatever the reasons behind this teaching, it is better to follow it than to debate it.

What strikes me as being of most concern here is not so much whether women are or are not to be affirmed as pastors or elders. On this issue each of us is responsible to examine the Word for guidance and follow what we believe to be God's will. I feel free to hold my own convictions while permitting others to hold theirs.

What most concerns me is that the debate about women leaders may cause us to lose sight of the fact that women *are* full and equal members of the Body: gifted, valued, ministering members. Another concern is that women may be tempted to make the issue of ordination a symbol of their acceptance as persons.

Either of these is tragic. On the one hand, the whole Church in our day needs desperately to affirm women as persons and open itself in every way to the ministry God intends to offer the whole Body through them. On the other hand, women and men both need to learn to live comfortably and affirmatively within whatever limitations God has placed on us. Each of us needs to develop a healthy self-esteem based not on position but on recognition of who we are in Christ. We do have God-given gifts with which to serve others.

If a woman *should* be disqualified from an office in the church, such a disqualification would in no way make her less significant as a sister, a person, or a unique and utterly vital member of the Body of Christ.

THE WELL-BEING OF THE WHOLE BODY

God's church is to glorify Him. It is meant to praise and worship its Lord and Head, Jesus Christ. It is also meant to build up and encourage its individual members. God desires that we be whole persons, and one of the reasons He has given us the church is to help our individual growth.

Not every member of a congregation will hold an office, but every member ought to be ministering to others and exercising the gifts he or she has been given.

On what basis do we choose leadership in the church? First, we look at the qualifications for leaders that Scripture sets out. Then we decide what gifts or abilities a position requires and look for people with the scriptural qualifications. We rid ourselves of the notion that church leadership is some sort of reward system or status symbol. Instead, we seek to affirm in men and women the gifts and callings that are theirs in Christ. We look to each other for leadership and learn to depend upon one another. The more we mature, the more we see how much we need the contributions of all the members of the body.

GOING DEEPER

to personalize

1. In this chapter the author has raised a number of questions about leadership. Read the pastoral Epistles again, looking for additional insights. Make a list of Paul's instructions about leaders.

2. If you were going to draw a church organizational chart that would incorporate all of the principles of leadership seen in these first four chapters, how would you draw it?

3. *For women:* Jot down your feelings about being a woman in your church. Do you feel accepted and valued as a person? If not, why not? How is either acceptance or nonacceptance communicated to you?

4. *For men:* Jot down your feelings about women in your church. Do you feel they are accepted or valued as persons? How do *you* communicate either acceptance or nonacceptance?

5. If you were responsible to decide what leadership roles in your church would be open to women, what would you decide? Be ready to explain your position.

BIBLE ALIVE SERIES

to probe

1. Respond to the following suggestion: "I don't see why we get all hot and bothered about women being on the church board. After all, our board really doesn't function like New Testament elders . . . I mean, we make decisions about the building and staff and spending and things like that, but spiritual oversight? Never! So why not have women? What's the difference?"

2. What can you find out about the theological (not cultural!) base Paul gives as his authority for restricting the elder or pastor office to men (1 Tim. 2:13-15). Research, and write a report on those brief, difficult verses.

Part Two
WARNINGS
2 Peter; Jude

5
2 Peter; Jude

TIMES OF STRESS

ONE OF MY FAMILY'S favorite TV series was "Space Family Robinson." The Robinsons, two passengers, and a friendly robot moved through the galaxy facing new threats each week. When the robot sensed some dark, mysterious force approaching, he would shout out, "Danger! Danger! Danger!"

In the last half of the first century, a threat far more sinister than those dreamed up by TV scriptwriters assailed the churches. The two short books of 2 Peter and Jude were written to sound an urgent alarm. As we move on in time (rather than space), we too need to be alerted to spiritual dangers and be prepared to meet them.

PETER AND JUDE

Who were these two men, and what was the historical context out of which they wrote?

Peter. The writer is, of course, that most prominent of the Twelve in the Gospels and the dominant figure in the early chapters of Acts. This is the second of two letters Peter wrote to the early church. It too is a "last days" letter, written at the end of the apostle's career.

According to the early church historian, Eusebius, Peter was martyred during Nero's persecutions (about A.D. 64-68). The letter was most likely written sometime between 66 and 68.

Heresy was clearly threatening the church, a heresy that challenged both doctrine and life-style. The books of 2 Peter, Jude, and 2 Timothy all contain clear teaching to combat this danger.

Jude. The writer's identification of himself in verse 1 and early church tradition have led to the conviction that Jude was a younger brother of the James who led the Jerusalem church, and thus was a younger brother of Jesus. It is very difficult to establish a date for Jude's short letter; suggested dates range from the late 60s to the 80s. The similarity with 2 Peter does not indicate that one copied the other. Instead it indicates how widespread the threat within the church had become, and that there was a common body of teaching to help congregations deal with such dangers.

PAUL'S CONCERN

Actually, early words of warning come from Paul in 2 Timothy, as well as from Jude and Peter. Paul warns Timothy of the teachers who have "wandered away from the truth" (2:18). He speaks of "terrible times" when "people will be lovers of themselves, lovers of money, boastful, proud, abusive, disobedient to their parents, ungrateful, unholy, without love, unforgiving, slanderous, without self-control, brutal, not lovers of the good, treacherous, rash, conceited, lovers of pleasure rather than lovers of God. Worst of all, they will retain "a form of godliness but denying its power" (3:1-5). While Timothy is to teach, correct, rebuke, and encourage with "great patience and careful instruction," he is also to realize that "the time will come when men will not put up with sound doctrine." They will instead shape doctrine to "suit their own desires" (4:2-3).

Times of stress are coming. Christians must recognize the signs of danger and be prepared to protect the purity of the church.

Persecution. When Paul, Peter, and Jude were writing these letters, danger signs were all around. Gentile nations had recognized Christianity as a faith distinct from Judaism, and the Jews had also become hateful and envious.

Other sources of opposition existed. In 2 Timothy Paul mentions Alexander the metalworker, who did him "a great deal of harm" (4:14). He was probably one of those whose living came from selling images of the gods. His livelihood was threatened by the growing Christian movement. Later even the butchers who sold meat for pagan sacrifices lost income because the people were forsaking the temples. The Emperor Nero would soon formally accuse Christians of "hatred of mankind" and put many of them to horrible deaths.

The Roman world was used to multiple faiths, all tolerated and existing side by side. Just as in the modern East a person may be both a Buddhist and Shintoist, the Roman world saw no problem with one person worshiping many gods or having several religions. Christians challenged this ethos. They refused to worship the emperor, which left them open to the charge of treason. They disturbed families with their insistence on total allegiance to one God. They refused to serve in the army and worship the legion eagles. All in all, they were a disruptive force in society. Often in the next decades local magistrates would initiate persecutions against these strange and unpopular people.

By the time of Trajan (about A.D. 100), problems caused for the empire by the spread of Christianity were serious. Pliny the Younger, governor of Bithynia around A.D. 112, executed a number of Christians. Then he wrote to the emperor asking for advice and instruction. Trajan instructed Pliny that those who admitted they were Christians and refused to give up their beliefs were to be executed. But the governor should not hunt Christians or accept anonymous accusations. And of course, any who gave up their faith and offered sacrifice to the emperor were to be released.

Within thirty years after Jude's and Peter's letters, Christians would face a world in which their faith itself was adequate cause for execution! Yet, as we read these "last word" letters of the Bible, we note a strange thing. *The danger that most concerns the apostles is not the danger from without.* They were confident that when believers were called before judges, God would stand beside them and give them the words for their defense (see Matt. 5:11, 44; 10:17-20; Luke 21:12-19; John 15:20-21; Acts 4:1-31). Throughout history, persecution has tended to strengthen rather than weaken the church. We see in fact that the great danger to Christians does not lie in the antagonism of outsiders at all.

Perversion. The great danger to the early church, as to us, is that what is central to the life of the corporate body can be perverted. Outsiders can never prevail against the Body of Christ. If the church is to remain strong and vital, it must be strong *within.* And inner strength depends on sustaining sound doctrine *and* a godly life-style.

Paul warns Timothy that opposition will come from "men of corrupt mind and counterfeit faith" (2 Tim. 3:8, RSV).

"There will be false teachers among you," Peter warns, "who will secretly introduce destructive heresies.... "Many will follow their shameful ways and bring the way of truth into disrepute" (2 Pet. 2:1-2).

Jude appeals to the church to contend for the faith, "for certain men . . . have secretly slipped in among you. They are godless men who change the grace of our God into a license for immorality and deny Jesus Christ our only Sovereign and Lord" (v. 4).

Each of these letters warns against the twin threats of false teaching and ungodly living *within* the church.

BIBLE ALIVE SERIES

TWIN THREATS

It helps us, in reading 2 Peter and Jude, to have an overview of the nature of the dangers. Let's look at each threat separately.

False teaching. There was a body of teaching or doctrine, entrusted by God to the prophets and apostles and recorded in the Scriptures (2 Pet. 3:2). A number of false teachings are mentioned in these letters and in 2 Timothy. Paul points out the mistaken belief that the resurrection of believers has already occurred. Peter warns against those who question Jesus' Second Coming and the certainty of the final judgment (2 Pet. 3:4-10). However, both Peter and Jude make it clear that the critical heresy that threatens the church has to do with who Jesus is. The godless men who secretly slip into the fellowship change God's grace and "deny Jesus Christ our only Sovereign and Lord" (Jude 4). Peter insists "we did not follow cleverly invented stories when we told you about the power and coming of our Lord Jesus Christ" (2 Pet. 1:16). The false teachers who secretly introduce destructive heresies are actually "denying the Sovereign Lord who bought them" (2 Pet. 2:1).

The crucial doctrinal danger is to deny Jesus as Sovereign Lord. We can understand why. The New Testament teaches that Jesus is the center of our faith, our life, and hope. Continuing in a personal relationship with Jesus is the only means we have to break the hold of sin or to give us freedom from tension, fear, or guilt. Christians have no power in themselves to produce a life of wholeness.

Any teaching or doctrine that denies Jesus Christ His primacy or reduces Him to less than God robs Him of His glory and us of our hope. Such a system of belief is what Paul calls a "counterfeit faith" (2 Tim. 3:8, RSV).

An ungodly life. While the necessity for sound doctrine is much in the minds of Peter and Jude in these warning letters, it's clear that they warn against moral decline even more. Just as Paul insisted that leaders be chosen for their spiritual maturity, so Jude and Peter warn against leaders whose lifestyles mark them off as perverters.

A number of terms and concepts here need explanation, lest we think an ungodly way of life is simply a life of gross and open sin. For instance, what is the "depraved mind" Paul speaks of (2 Tim. 3:8)? And what are the "passions" or "evil desires" that find such frequent mention in these letters?

The Greek word translated "mind" is *nous* and is much more than intelligence or the organ of thought. Greek scholars point out that this term refers to the sum total of the mental and moral state of being. We might call the biblical "mind" an attitude, perspective, way of thinking, or approach to life.

Is there a distinctive Christian life perspective? Of course there is. We are to find worth and importance in persons rather than things. We are to love, not use or abuse others. The Christian perspective measures material against eternal values and finds the unseen more real than the visible. The Christian outlook on life enjoys holiness and finds sin uncomfortable; it rejects instinctual responses in favor of self-control. By loving God and others, a Christian finds a fulfillment that no other focus for life could possibly bring.

Anything that draws us from this distinctive Christian perspective on life is a dangerous threat to the church. Only in building our lives on God's values can we find the holiness that gives the Christian fellowship vitality and power.

What may draw us into the world of illusion that is secular society's "mind"? Jude and Peter speak often of passions and instinctual desires. It would be a mistake to understand only these as sexual terms. The word translated "passions" or "desires" is the Greek word *epithumia*. In classical Greek the term is morally neutral: it simply means "desire." It could mean having a longing for something worthwhile, or it could imply desiring a forbidden object.

When a person enters into a friendship with Jesus, he gets a new life in which the old desires, thoughts, and choices are to be transformed. The "desires" (*epithumia*) that concern Paul, Peter, and Jude are leftover drives and stirring passions of our old way of life. Peter identifies them as "the evil desires you had when you lived in ignorance" (1 Pet. 1:14). We are not to conform to them or be "enslaved by all kinds of passions and pleasures" (Titus 3:3).

It is not wrong for a Christian to have feelings and wants. After all, God Himself promises that He will give us "the desires of our heart" (Ps. 47:4; see also Ps. 20:4; 21:2; 145:19). We are free to move toward that which we want deeply; and as we live with God, He Himself will cause us to desire His best (see Psalm 103:5).

One difficult lesson for an astronaut to learn is that his old physical reactions, adapted to earth's gravity pull, are inappropriate in weightlessness. He takes a normal step and bounces off the floor. He needs to learn to shuffle his feel to keep contact between magnetic shoes and the metal spacecraft. He grasps a wrench to turn a bolt and finds himself, not the bolt, moved by the force he exerts. In his new environment his old instinctive reactions are wrong.

The Christian too lives in a new environment: a kingdom ruled over by God's dear Son. The desires that shaped our perspective before we knew Christ produce the wrong reactions now. Thus Peter and Jude warn us against men who claim to be spiritual leaders but whose life-styles indicate they "follow the corrupt desire of their sinful natures" (2 Pet. 2:10) and react "like brute beasts, creatures of instinct" (2:12), their personalities shaped by the *epithumia* of fallen humanity.

The real threat to the church is not persecution from without but corruption from within. How can we recognize this danger? Corruption from within involves a desertion of sound doctrine. When we "reinterpret" or reject the apostolic teaching recorded in Scripture, and especially when we deny the central teaching of Scripture about the person and work of Jesus, we wander from the truth and place our generation in jeopardy.

But corruption from within also involves a retreat

BIBLE ALIVE SERIES

from a holy life. When we begin to respond to life situations as instinct tells us, motivated by the old *epithumia* that gripped us before we knew Jesus, our whole perspective becomes warped. The Bible says it: "Do not conform any longer to the pattern of this world, but be transformed by the renewing of your mind (*nous*)" (Rom. 12:2). We must understand that a commitment to both sound doctrine and godly life is essential, not only for church leaders, but for all believers. Any retreat from either, and we hear, through Peter and Jude, God's own danger alarm.

GOING DEEPER

to personalize

1. Read through both 2 Peter and Jude quickly several times. Then choose one of the following topics and write down all you can discover about it from these two brief letters:
- characteristics of false teachers
- appeal of false teaching
- false doctrines that were being taught
- our response to the false teachers
- defense against attacks from within

2. We noted that developing a Christian mind (perspective or attitude toward life) is essential to our Christian growth. How can we tell whether a person in our congregation is simply a young Christian whose attitudes reflect this need to grow, or is a false teacher against whom the Bible warns? How might we respond to an immature person differently than we would to a false teacher?

3. Can a false teacher be doctrinally correct and yet perverted in mind and life-style? Can you think of some leadership decisions in your church that were made on the basis of the old passions of human nature? What desires (*epithumia*) listed in 2 Peter do you think still affect the decisions you make? Choose one of these desires and illustrate its possible impact on leadership in the local church.

to probe
1. Research the later first century. What kind of attacks on the faith from within does church history record? What kind can be deducted from Jude and 2 Peter?
2. If you were leading a local congregation today, how would you guard the congregation against the dangers of which Jude and Peter warn?
3. Find and list at least fifteen common links between Jude's twenty-five-verse exposition and 2 Peter. Then choose one of the common items to examine in a two- to three-page paper.

6
Jude; 2 Peter

HERESY!

IT'S A FRIGHTENING WORD. Throughout history many who were labeled heretics have been tortured and put to death or driven from their homes. Sometimes those called heretical by the majority have proven to be the true believers!

What is heresy, and who is the heretic? How is the church to guard against heresy? And how is the heretic to be treated?

Perhaps these seem to be almost irrelevant questions. Our culture values tolerance so much that taking a stand for truth or righteousness is foreign to our society's way of thinking. In much the same way, the exclusiveness of early Christianity, with its insistence that Christ alone saved, grated on the values of the first-century world.

Certainly we don't execute heretics today, and we don't persecute those who differ from us. But how do we recognize heresy? And how should we respond when false teachers, like those against whom Jude and Peter warn, creep into the church and introduce their "destructive heresies" (2 Pet. 2:1)?

ANALYSIS OF HERESY

The Random House Unabridged dictionary defines heresy as an "opinion or doctrine at variance with the orthodox or accepted doctrine." In Roman Catholic tradition, the reference continues, a heretic is "a baptised Roman Catholic who willfully and persistently rejects any article of faith." Both these definitions focus attention on doctrine, but in Scripture the word has a wider application.

The Greek word from which *heretic* derives is *hairesis* and means "sect, party, or school" (as of a school of philosophy). It was used of the "party of the Pharisees" in Acts 15:5, which Paul calls "the strictest sect of our religion" (Acts 16:5). In the Christian movement it came to refer to a dissenting faction a group holding some opinion or dogma that marked them off from the rest of the body (1 Cor. 11:18-19; Gal. 5:20). In essence, heretics seem to be individuals within the church who hold to some way of thinking or living that sets them off from scriptural doctrine, life-style, and fellowship.

As we saw in our last chapter, factions may develop over various teachings such as the Resurrection or the Second Coming, but the truly critical element in "destructive heresies" has to do with the Person of Christ. No doctrine that fails to give Jesus preeminence as God and Sovereign Lord can be considered Christian.

But heresy also involves variation in life-style.

God's people are called to holiness. When we desert Christian attitudes and values, turning to a licentious following of old impulses and desires, we have also fallen into heresy. We have become a faction, dividing the body.

Characteristics of false teachers. Paul instructed Timothy and Titus to officially recognize those in the churches who had matured in the faith and who demonstrated their reliability by adhering to sound doctrine and by living exemplary Christian lives. Now Peter and Jude identify false teachers by the opposite characteristics.

False teachers claim a special knowledge or interpretation that differs from the common core of belief in the Christian community. They charge that doctrine recorded in Scripture is "cleverly invented stories" (2 Pet. 1:16). They also reject the authority of Scripture and the present leaders of the Christian community (2 Pet. 2:10; Jude 8, 10). False teachers can be recognized by their insistence that they alone have the truth. Sooner or later in their denial of apostolic teaching they attack the person of Jesus and seek to rob Him of His centrality.

False teachers also claim freedom to live a life moved by the old passions. They are competitive. Rather than serving, they use and exploit others. They rationalize their immorality and "are grumblers and faultfinders; they follow their own evil desires; they boast about themselves and flatter others for their own advantage" (Jude 16). At every point their characters lack the qualities Paul says are to be found in spiritual leaders.

Jude warns that "some have secretly slipped in among you" (v. 4), which implies that neither the false teaching nor the sinful life-style may be evident initially. No wonder Paul warns that those considered for leadership "must first be tested" and then serve an apprenticeship as deacons "if there is nothing against them" (1 Tim. 3:10). He points out that while "the sins of some men are obvious," the "sins of others trail behind them" (1 Tim. 5:24). Because flaws of character are not always readily apparent, selecting church leaders should never be a hasty or careless process.

Appeal of false teachers. How does it happen that those who introduce heresies all too often find followers within the church?

First, it's clear that their appeal is to the immature: those who are not deeply grounded in sound doctrine, and who need to grow in the Christian lifestyle. No wonder Peter begins his letter with the exhortation to "make every effort to add to your faith goodness; and to goodness, knowledge; and to knowledge, self-control; and to self-control, perseverance; and to perseverance, godliness; and to godliness, brotherly kindness; and to brotherly kindness, love. For if you possess these qualities in increasing measure, they will keep you from being ineffective and unproductive in your knowledge of our Lord Jesus Christ" (2 Pet. 1:5-8). Growth in the disciplines of the Christian life must follow our initial step of faith if we are to resist the lure of the false teacher.

But what is the appeal of false teachers? In part it

is an appeal to pride in a superior and special knowledge that sets us apart from others. "They may believe *that,* but we know better!" But the main thrust of heresy's appeal seems to lie in its promise of freedom to indulge our instinctual desires. "They mouth empty, boastful words," Peter says, "and, by appealing to the lustful desires of sinful human nature, they entice people who are just escaping from those who live in error. They promise them freedom, while they themselves are slaves of depravity—for a man is a slave to whatever has mastered him" (2 Pet. 2: 18-19). Certainly it is inviting to "follow mere natural instincts" (Jude 19). It's hard to surrender our desires to God for reshaping and deny ourselves the sensations our old way of life has taught us to crave. The false teacher justifies any and all behavior by corrupting God's grace into a "license for immorality" (Jude 4).

Some time ago on a talk show a young challenger insisted to Billy Graham that sexual intercourse was the same as a ham sandwich. Sex and hunger are both natural desires, he explained; when you feel a desire, you satisfy it. After all, if God has made an experience pleasurable, then it must be good.

The false teacher seeks to encourage within the church a passion for pleasure that draws people away from the life of holiness and self-control to which the Christian is called. Some will become "lovers of pleasure rather than lovers of God," Paul warns (2 Tim. 3:4).

The Christian life is not a miserable withdrawal or a dreary denial of every pleasant thing. We are to find our pleasure in what God calls holy, not in distorted passions and desires. Scripture promises, "In thy right hand are pleasures for evermore" (Psalm 16:11).

Any invitation to share a special revelation that the rest of the church does not possess, or any promise of freedom to indulge our every "natural" desire with God's blessing, should be a warning to us. We may have met a false teacher who seeks to shatter the oneness of the body in which God has placed us.

Response to false teachers. Jude tells us that we are to "contend" for the faith. To some in history, to contend for the faith meant to attack those who deviated from sound doctrine. Such an approach led to men and women burned at the stake, wars fought, and inquisitions fashioned in order to enforce conformity. Yet there is no hint in the Bible of a crusade to exclude the deviate. How then do we "contend"? Here are several principles from these letters to help us.

- *Stand on unshakable foundations.* Paul reminds Timothy that in spite of doctrinal challenges from Hymenaeus and Philetus, who have wandered away from the truth, "God's solid foundation stands firm, sealed with this inscription: 'The Lord knows those who are his,' and, 'Everyone who confesses the name of the Lord must turn away from wickedness' " (2 Tim. 2:17-19).

We may proceed with the firm conviction that, while we may be uncertain who belongs to the Lord, He knows. But at the same time, one who confesses the name of the Lord "must turn from wickedness." *Open sin* requires judgment and discipline in the Christian community.

- *Give gentle instruction.* Rather than trying to silence the false teacher with shouting, Paul instructs, "Don't have anything to do with foolish and stupid arguments" (2 Tim. 2:23). Debate may be exciting, but it is not productive. Instead, the leaders of the Christian community are to "gently instruct" those who oppose (2 Tim. 2:25). We prayerfully communicate sound doctrine "in the hope that God will give them a change of heart leading them to a knowledge of the truth, and that they will come to their senses and escape from the trap of the devil, who has taken them captive to do his will" (2 Tim. 2:25-26).

The fleshly approach of the false teacher is to attack, challenge authority, ridicule, strike out, and abuse. The Christian must respond with love, recognizing that he is not battling against an enemy but *for* a fellow human being. In this spiritual confrontation, the warfare is between God and Satan. As for us, we are to simply "be merciful to those who doubt, snatch others from the fire and save them; to others show mercy mixed with fear—hating even the clothing stained by corrupted flesh" (v. 22).

- *Depend on divine judgment.* Our response to heretical challenges to the Christian community should not be confused with compromise. There can be no retreat from truth nor a withdrawal of love. God "knows how to rescue godly men from trials and to hold the uprighteous for the day of judgment" (2 Pet. 2:9). Both in this life and the life to come, the Lord involves Himself directly in the judgment of those who persistently rebel against Him. We can trust the false teacher to God and be free to concentrate on building ourselves up in the faith.

Protection against false teachers. These letters not only warn us of dangers from within the church, but also describe safeguards. If we as individuals and fellowships are firmly committed to these principles, we can be confident that we will be immune to any heresies that might appear:

- Be aware of the characteristics of false teachers and false teaching so we can recognize and reject them.
- Follow only leaders who meet the qualifications given by Paul in his letters to Timothy and Titus.
- Study to understand the apostolic doctrine preserved for us in Scripture.
- Commit ourselves to the holy way of life and unique values to which God calls us in His Word.

2 PETER

To see even more fully God's plan of protection for His own, we'll briefly trace the thought of 2 Peter.

Peter begins by reminding us that God "has given us everything we need for life and godliness through our knowledge of him who called us by his own glory and goodness" (1:3). Jesus is sufficient; we don't have to look for something beyond a relationship with Him. Chapter two is devoted to a description to false teachers and their end. Chapters one and three encourage and exhort believers, showing us how to avoid the growing dangers from within.

Growth vital (2 Pet. 1:5-11). The faith that brings us into relationship with God marks only the beginning of our life with Him. We are to concentrate on maturing in character so that we are no longer attracted by the false teacher's alluring promise of "liberty." "If you do these things," Peter says, "you will never fall" (v. 10).

Apostolic teaching trustworthy (2 Pet. 1:12-21). Peter reminds the readers that the sound doctrine of the Church is rooted in reality. The apostles did not relate "cleverly invented stories" but communicated historical facts to which they were eyewitnesses. All they report is in harmony with the prophetic Word of the Old Testament. The two Testaments stand as one, giving sure witness to the foundation truths of the Church.

In this passage one phrase of verse 20 has been puzzling. The New International Version translates it "no prophecy of Scripture came about by the prophet's own interpretation," while the Revised Standard Version, in harmony with the King James, renders it "no prophecy of Scripture is a matter of one's own interpretation." The original Greek permits either of these renderings, and both have suggestive implications. In the first case we are reminded that it is God who speaks through His prophets and apostles. The Word is trustworthy because it is His own. In the second we are reminded that a false teacher may quote Scripture but give his own interpretation that will differ from what the whole Bible teaches and from what the Church has historically taught. When a sect, such as Jehovah's Witnesses, presents its own distinctive interpretation of Bible passages to deny the deity of Christ, we can look to the Word itself to refute the heresy. We can also look to the Church as a whole, past and present, to see the voice of faith universally affirming that those verses teach that Jesus *is* God, fully human, yet one with the Father from all eternity.

While there have been, and are, differences in interpretation of minor details of doctrine, the core of apostolic faith, as represented in the Apostles' Creed, has the joyful affirmation of the Church universal.

Judgment coming (2 Pet. 3). This chapter is a striking affirmation of the trustworthiness of God's Word. Looking across the coming generations Peter warns of scoffers, who will doubt Christ's return and question the certainty of judgment. They will insist that "since our fathers died, everything goes on as it has since the beginning of creation" (v. 4). Yet God *did* intervene in the past to destroy the world in judgment, and this same God will intervene again, to destroy the works of human society (3:10-13).

We are not to let scoffers shake us from our certainty that the Lord will keep His promises. Because this universe will pass out of existence, we are to concentrate on that which is eternal. "So then, dear friends," Peter urges, "since you are looking forward to this, make every effort to be found spotless, blameless, and at peace with him" (3:14). As we concentrate every effort on pleasing Him who has delivered us into the Kingdom of Jesus Christ, we will be untouched by the lure of false teachers. They offer only the fleeting pleasures of a world that will someday flare up and then burn out.

GOING DEEPER

to personalize

1. Write your own definition of heresy. Then check it with the chapter and other reference books.
2. Take the following quick quiz. List one or two answers to each:
  (a) What is a characteristic of false teachers?
  (b) What is a characteristic of false teaching?
  (c) What is a correct response to false teaching?
  (d) What is a protection against false teaching?
3. Do you believe you have ever been under false teaching or a false teacher? Describe the situation briefly.
4. Reread 2 Peter and Jude carefully, seeing what you can add to the author's discussion of false teaching.
5. Jude's closing doxology (vv. 24-25) is especially significant in view of his subject. Read it, and meditate on what it means to you.

to probe

1. Peter and Jude both mention historic examples of false teaching and false teachers. Locate these references, and do a study of the Old Testament

contexts. What insights do these illustrations provide?

2. Look through church history and find one classic example of heresy. How did it follow or differ from the pattern laid out by Peter and Jude? How did people in that day respond to it? What was its end?

3. Or, look for a contemporary false teacher or heretical movement. How should the church and Christians today respond? How *are* believers responding?

Part Three
A LIFE OF LOVE
1, 2, and 3 John

7
1 John 1:1–2:2

THE DISCIPLE JESUS LOVED

IT'S QUITE EASY to sense the personalities of Peter and Paul from material in the New Testament. In the Gospels bombastic Peter blurts out his first thoughts; in Acts a matured and Spirit-filled Peter dominates early church history. And Paul speaks so openly of his feelings and motives that sometimes we're embarrassed by his totally honest revelations.

But it's hard for us to visualize John, so humble that in his Gospel he cannot bear to name himself. With quiet joy he refers obliquely to "the disciple whom Jesus loved" (John 21:7). We know that John was one of the inner circle along with his brother James and Peter. We know that at the Last Supper John found a place as close to Jesus as possible. But what else do we know about this quiet apostle? And what do we know about his writings?

JOHN AND HIS WRITINGS

The man. When John and his brother James, the

sons of Zebedee, began to follow Jesus, they were apparently quite young and passionate. Once the disciples were passing through Samaria on the way to Jerusalem. James and John went on ahead to find lodging in a village. When the Samaritans, who hated the Jews as much as they were hated, learned the party was traveling to Jerusalem, they refused them shelter. Furious, James and John confronted Jesus. "Lord," they asked, "do you want us to call fire down from heaven to destroy them?" (Luke 9:54.) Their nickname was appropriate: "Thunderers."

Another time the disciples saw a man driving out demons in Jesus' name, but the man was not one of their company. "We told him to stop," John reported, "because he was not one of us" (Mark 9:38). John was again corrected by Jesus because his zeal had missed the spirit of his Master.

A final Gospel incident (Matt. 20:20-28) completes John's portrait. He and his brother whisper privately to their mother. Shortly she approaches Jesus. Could the places of authority at Jesus' right and left hand be reserved for her sons when the Lord takes power in His Kingdom? Jesus explains to the mother and to the two sons that He did not have the authority to grant such a request. Later the other disciples hear of the pair's attempt to gain advantage and react with understandable anger. Then Jesus explains to the Twelve that greatness in His Kingdom is not found in authority but in servanthood: a servanthood far removed from the self-concerned attitude of James and John.

We can understand John; we've all known (and

possibly been) such firebrands. We understand his quickness to take offense and the anger that urges him to strike back. We understand the pride that holds others at arm's length. We understand the drive to succeed, the hunger to be somebody and gain a high place even at the expense of friends. We understand all this because these are the motivating passions (*epithumia*) in our world. These are the desires the "last word" letters encourage us to replace with a set of values summed up in the concept of holiness. Yes, we understand young John only too well: he's so much us!

But when we come to John's writings, we meet a different man. We meet a man whose favorite word is *love,* a man who is gentle, so selfless that he hardly mentions himself or his feelings, except as they relate to the needs of the men and women to whom he ministers. We meet a man who *is* transformed, who demonstrates in his own personality the Bible promise that we can be changed by beholding Jesus (2 Cor. 3:12).

John emphasizes that Jesus loved him in the days before he grew to Christian maturity; thus he identifies himself as "the disciple whom Jesus loved." What a message for you and me: Jesus loves and accepts us no matter what our stage of growth. Jesus' new life *will* grow within us and, as John, we will become more and more like our Lord.

John's writings. John's epistles were probably written from Ephesus and circulated in the churches in Asia. They were immediately accepted by the whole Church: we even have evidence of an exegesis (study and explanation) of John's Gospel from as early as A.D. 150.

Like Peter and Jude, John counsels the church about dangers from within. He warns against antichrists who are trying to lead believers astray. Like the others, John identifies the spirit of antichrist with the denial that "Jesus Christ has come in the flesh" (1 John 4:2). The person of Jesus is the central doctrinal truth, and a relationship with Him, who *is* God, is the irreplaceable essence of our Christian experience. He also reminds us that sin by any name is the devil's work: we are not to be moved by appeals to our old passions.

1 JOHN 1:1—2:2

The heresy emerging in the days of Peter and Jude was an even greater danger by John's time. As competing teachers introduced conflicting doctrines, many Christians became confused about who was the false teacher and who was the true. Confusion also arose as the drive for holiness brought an unexpected reaction: those who slipped into sin began to wonder if they still had a personal relationship with God.

John focuses on the doubts, fears, and uncertainties that well up in us as we try to follow Christ yet often find ourselves stumbling and unsure.

Fellowship and joy (1 John 1:1-3). John immediately shares with us his deeply personal concern; he writes in order "that you also may have fellowship with us. And our fellowship is with the Father and with his

Son, Jesus Christ" (v. 3). "Fellowship" is the Greek word *koinonia*. It's a word of intimacy and means "communion; close relationship; participation; sharing." John's desire for us is what we ourselves yearn for: a warm, comfortable relationship with God in which we're aware of being close to Him in heart and mind.

John has seen in the historical Jesus (1:1-2) the reality of *life*. In Jesus eternal life entered time, and through Jesus John personally experiences that fellowship he desires for all of us. We can almost picture the old man, deeply aware of how close he now stands beside his Lord, beckoning you and me to come closer and share with him that intimate relationship with the Father and Son that makes joy complete.

Walking in light (1 John 1:5-7). But how can we have fellowship with God? John's first answer is simple. God is light, and if we walk in light, we will have fellowship.

Often when John speaks of light (and he uses the term thirty-three times in his writings), he is quoting Jesus: "I am the light of the world. Whoever follows me will never walk in darkness, but will have the light of life" (John 8:12; see 9:5; 12:46). The essential nature of God as light sets God apart from man. Man's sinful condition has made the world lie in darkness. Even worse, "men loved darkness instead of light, because their deeds were evil" (John 3:19). Confronted with the nature of God, men twist and struggle to turn away from such holiness. "Light" and "darkness" are *moral* terms in John's writings.

The character of God is expressed as light; the character of sinful man is expressed as darkness.

So in his first letter John confronts us with a disconcerting reality. If we are to be comfortable with God and live in intimate fellowship with Him, we must "walk in the light as he is in the light" (v. 7). Our values, our behavior, our attitudes, our commitments must be in harmony with God's character rather than with the natural *epithumia* of fallen humanity.

But this seems to raise a terrible barrier. If we must walk in light to have fellowship, how can we, who feel sin's pull and all too often give in to temptations, ever be comfortable with God? Isn't each sin a retreat to darkness? If sinlessness is the avenue to fellowship, who then can stand in the presence of God?

But John is *not* talking of sinlessness: "If we walk in the light... the blood of Jesus, his Son, purifies us from every sin" (1:7). Even those walking in the light need forgiveness and cleansing from sins they commit. While it is possible for us in Christ not to sin, we can never claim that it is impossible to sin.

John's primary target here seems to be those who "claim to have fellowship with him yet walk in the darkness" (1:6). These men and women speak glowingly of their closeness to God and the fellowship they enjoy and yet make a practice of sin. Their life-style is not godly; it is patterned after the ways of the false teachers described by Jude and Peter. No one who makes a practice of sin can claim fellowship with God: God's nature is light, not darkness. Those who walk in light as He is in the light may fall, but they will quickly turn back from that old life-style to find forgiveness in Jesus.

We might sum up John's teaching this way: if the direction of your life is toward the source of light, you will find forgiveness for your failures and inadequacies. But if the direction of your life is toward the darkness, then you may be sure you have nothing in common with God.

Confession (1 John 1:8-10). John's readers were confused by two false teachings. The first was the claim that those who choose sin's life-style can maintain fellowship with God. This John labels as a lie (v. 6). The second claim was by those who said they were without sin (v. 8). They based their right of fellowship with God on the belief that they matched God in His moral perfection! John calls this claim self-deceit: "We deceive ourselves and the truth is not in us" (v. 8).

Truth and falsehood are not related so much to the trustworthiness of the teller as they are to correspondence with reality. The problem with the claim to sinlessness is not that the motives of the claimant are unpure. His or her report may be made with honest conviction. But the report of sinlessness is mistaken; it does not correspond with reality! "We deceive ourselves and the truth is not in us."

What is the reality of sin for the Christian? The simple fact is that while in His death Jesus dealt fully with sin, the sin nature within us is not eradicated. The ingrained responses still tug. We still experience pride, lust, anger, hatred, and fear. The capacity to sin remains ours and will be an ever-present burden until we find our full release in resurrection.

But the capacity to sin, and even the temptation to sin, are not really the issue in the Christian life. What is at issue are our *choices*. While we can feel the old passions stirring, we also have a new appreciation for godliness. We *want* to be like Jesus! Now two sets of desires war within us, and we have been given the freedom to choose. We can walk toward light and live in the radiance shed by the living Word. Or we can turn our backs and chase off into the darkness after the illusive pleasures of sin. The choices we make, not the temptations we experience, are what move us into darkness or into light.

But again John is sensitive. Men and women who turn toward the light, and begin that hesitant journey toward holiness, find their sinful "deeds will be exposed" (John 3:20-21). In the radiance of the light of Jesus, we become aware of pools of darkness in ourselves. Things we did that before seemed natural and proper become tawdry and shameful. Motives we suppressed come to light. The action we justified we see to be a petty release of antagonisms. Our drive to succeed is recognized as materialism that has pushed aside the needs of our family and replaced the value of persons with the love of money.

The more we live in the light Jesus sheds, the more aware we become of how unlike God we are. Rather than feeling comfortable in His presence, we pull back in shame and hopelessness, deciding we are forever separated from Him. Or, unable to face the reality, we deceive ourselves and deny the blemishes that surface. "My sin is gone," we insist. And since pettiness and antagonism are wrong, we rechristen our reactions "righteous indignation." We dare not acknowledge our materialism and distorted values, so we justify our drive to succeed by the money we can give to support missions. Closing our eyes to reality, we wander through life, insisting on our sinlessness and yet wondering why we have only an aching void inside rather than fellowship's joy.

But what's the alternative? How can a sinful and sinning human being have a joyful and comfortable relationship with a holy God? John says, "If we confess our sins, he is faithful and just and will forgive us our sins and purify us from all unrighteousness" (1:9). *The basis of our fellowship with God is not our sinlessness, but His forgiveness.*

Let's remember the development of John's explanation before going on. You and I are invited to live our lives in intimate relationship with God, in comfortable closeness and joy. The key to experiencing this kind of fellowship is to walk in light, not darkness. Some may claim fellowship while obviously choosing sin. They lie. Others may claim fellowship on the basis of having achieved sinlessness. They deceive themselves. The reality is that fellowship can be ours in spite of our imperfection!

To have fellowship involves choosing a basic direction *toward* godliness; walking *into* the light, we can see God and reality. We will also become aware of our sins and failures. We will become aware of all that God still has to do in our personality to make us truly godly.

The apostle of love, who was once an angry youth, knew that God's remedy for our sins is to confess (acknowledge) them (1:9). Instead of hiding our deep needs, we acknowledge to God the realities revealed by His light, and He "will forgive us our sins and purify us from all unrighteousness." God's forgiving grace will remove every barrier between the believer and God, even that of remembered guilt, so that we can be comfortable in the very presence of our Lord.

One last important promise is given us by John. God will not only forgive us as we acknowledge the sins we discover, but He will also purify us. God will touch our motives and desires, and He will gradually reshape us. Like John himself, as we walk into the light of Jesus, we will gradually lose the old anger and drive for prestige and will become men and women who love.

A dangerous promise? (1 John 2:1-2). Some reading John's letter were sure to object to his teaching: "If we know we can be forgiven" they ask, "then why not sin? If that's all there is to fellowship, why make the effort to follow Jesus?" The objectors of course misunderstood: only the person who *wants* to live in darkness will pervert the promise of forgiveness into a license for sin.

John is writing to help us avoid sin. "But if anybody does sin, we have one who speaks to the Father in our defense—Jesus Christ, the Righteous One. He is the atoning sacrifice for our sins, and not only for ours but also for the sins of the whole world" (2:1-2).

How completely sufficient is the blood of Jesus Christ! Enough for the whole world, it is surely enough for you and me. Let us then go on boldly with full confidence in Him, walking into the Light.

GOING DEEPER

to personalize
1. What kind of person do you think John was? Jot down your impressions from what you have read in the Gospels or this chapter.
2. How do you think you are like or unlike John? Be as specific as you can about personality differences.
3. Read and reread 1 John 1:1—2:2. How would John's teaching meet your needs if you were one of the following persons?
• *Myra.* You always felt like a failure. Never did well in school. Boys stayed away from you in droves. You have the feeling no one really likes you. You thought that becoming a Christian was the answer. But now you've failed so many times to be a "good Christian" that you're close to despair.
• *Jana.* You've never failed. Always got top grades. Popular. You graduated third in your law school class and are moving up in your law firm. As a new Christian, you're as determined not to fail in your faith as you have been in your other efforts. In fact, you won't even *admit* the possibility of failure.
• *Sally.* You're just an average person. Win a few,

BIBLE ALIVE SERIES

lose a few. Of course, now you've got a really important goal: to live close to God. And that's what's bothering you a little bit. You're *so* average. How can you be special enough to come close to Him?

to probe
Using a concordance, study one of the following words. Look up every usage in John's writings and write a paper on what you discover. The words: *Light. Darkness. Life. Truth.*

8
1 John 2:3–3:10

TO KNOW HIM

THE DEEPEST DESIRE the New Testament writers expressed was not for our personal growth or even transformation. It was, in Paul's words, to know Christ: "I want to know Christ and the power of his resurrection and the fellowship of sharing in his sufferings, becoming like him in his death, and so, somehow, to attain to the resurrection from the dead" (Phil. 3:10). Knowing Jesus opens the door to a present experience of resurrection power. It lifts us out of our deadness and mirrors eternal life in this world of space and time and history. And it all hinges on knowing Jesus.

But how can we be *sure* that we know Him?

Part of our problem is that we get confused over the meanings of the word *know*. We use this simple word so many ways. For instance,

- "I know that" means I have information.
- "I know all about bass" may be a claim that I can catch them.

- "I know Henry" may express friendship, acquaintance, or simply ability to identify a person in a crowd.
- "I know Plato" probably is a claim to understand or to be acquainted with his philosophy.
- "I know what you mean" can be an expression of sympathy.

We could go on giving the word slightly different slants. So it's not enough to say, "Knowing Jesus is important." We need to grasp the meaning of *know* when we apply it to a relationship with the Lord.

The *Dictionary of New Testament Theology* points out that the Greek word used by John, *ginosko,* has a basic meaning "of grasping the full reality and nature of the object under consideration. It is thus distinguished from mere opinion, which may grasp the object half-correctly, inadequately or even falsely." When John says, "We can be sure we know him . . ." (1 John 2: 3), he is about to show us how we can be confident that we are not half-correct, or mistaken, or inadequate in our knowing of Jesus.

Like *light* and *truth,* this word *know* is a favorite of John's. *To know* is used 221 times in the New Testament, 82 times by John (Paul used it only 52 times!).

Each New Testament writer, while often using *know* in ways common to the contemporary Greek usage, adds a special dimension drawn from the Old Testament concept of knowledge. There *know* expresses a personal relationship between the one who knows and the one knowing. John's emphasis is consistently on this kind of knowing. He is not so concerned that we know in the sense of having information about God, but he cares deeply that we know in the sense of *having a close personal relationship* with God through Jesus Christ.

John wrote to people who knew *about* Jesus but who weren't sure they knew Him. We know *about* Jesus, but our grasp of truth may be incomplete or we may have been misled by a false system of doctrine. How can we be sure that in spite of gaps in our understanding we have a close personal relationship with Him?

INNER EVIDENCE OF RELATIONSHIP
1 John 2:3-17

John launches into an explanation of how we can be sure, not theoretically but experientially, that we know Jesus, so we can be free from nagging doubts and fears.

We respond to His commands (1 John 2:3-6). Jesus said, "My sheep listen to my voice; I know them, and they follow me" (John 10:27). Those who belong to Jesus are responsive to His voice.

It's important not to misunderstand here. John does not suggest that relationship with God is *established* by obedience; rather, that relationship is *demonstrated* by obedience.

Sometimes people claim to know God but are unresponsive to His Word and His way of life. Such a person may possess accurate information about God and may be able to debate fine points of theology. Such a person may have memorized much of the Bible and regularly be in church. But unresponsiveness to God's voice shows the claim "I know Him" to be a lie. Relationship is demonstrated by walking "as Jesus did" (v. 6).

The central command (1 John 2:7-11). This idea of responsiveness can be distorted into a legalism in which the list of do's and don't's grows longer. We try to measure our relationship with God as we do the temperature . . . by degrees.

To avoid this error, John quickly notes a central command from which all else flows. That command has been known and revealed through both the Testaments but has been given fresh meaning in Jesus' coming. Jesus calls us to "Love one another. As I have loved you, so you must love one another" (John 13:34). John says that one who hates his brother cannot be walking in the light (John 13:34).

If you or I wonder if we're really responsive to Jesus' voice, we don't have to measure ourselves against a list of things we do or don't do to please Him. All we have to do is look within to see if we are reaching out to care for our fellow Christians.

The listeners (1 John 2:12-14). John seems to have more confidence in the people he writes to than they do themselves. He doesn't question their relationship with Jesus. He is sure that they do know Him and that they can live in fellowship with God.

John has reasons for his confidence:

• These little children have made an initial commitment to Jesus, and their sins have been forgiven.

• These fathers have lived in relationship with a God who has demonstrated Himself to be stable and trustworthy from the beginning of the universe.

• These young men have been challenged in their faith by the evil one, and God's strength and His Word in them has enabled them to overcome the threat.

These people can take the test John suggests. They can examine themselves and discover that they are responsive to Jesus' voice; they have begun to love. These inner drawings toward Jesus help us to be sure that we do know him.

Divided hearts (1 John 2:15-17). John has helped us look within to discover evidence of the reality of our relationship with Jesus. Now John warns that in order to love and respond to God, we must stop acting from the motives that reflect the world's value system.

Again John has given a common word a distinctive moral slant. *Kosmos* in Greek can mean the universe itself, the planet on which we live, or mankind. In a moral sense, however, *world* refers to the created universe and mankind *as fallen:* "As that which is at enmity with God; lost in sin; wholly at odds with anything divine; ruined and depraved."[2] This world, John says later (1 John 5:19), "is under the control of the evil one." The values and attitudes that characterize the world—"cravings of sinful man, the lust of his eyes and his pride in possessions" (2:16) do not come from God.

A Christian cannot live with a divided heart, responding one moment out of love for God and at the next turning to the world for pleasure. If we want to demonstrate (to ourselves as well as to Him) that we know Him, we need to make a clear-cut commitment to do the will of God rather than respond to the world's *epithumia*.

WARNING AGAINST ANTICHRIST
1 John 2:18-27

John has helped us see inner, subjective evidence that we know Jesus. You and you alone know if you are responsive to God's voice. A new Christian might be responsive, but as yet show little change in lifestyle. And you and you alone know if you are beginning to love. If you find the stirrings of obedience and love within yourself, then you can have confidence that you know Jesus.

But what are the objective criteria? How about those who claim to be Christians, and even to be teachers, but who instead are antichrists? How can we recognize false teachers and false prophets?

John gives several principles to guide us. First, they "went out from us" (v. 19). The false teacher comes into the fellowship, begins to teach his lies and, when he cannot influence the whole group to follow him, takes the little band he has deceived and starts his own sect or movement. Watch out for those who would divide and separate Christ's people. They go out "because they did not really belong to us" (v. 19).

Second, they deny Jesus was the Christ. Rejecting the Son, they reject the Father also. Jude and Peter have stressed as well that the false teacher sooner or later distorts the Bible's teaching of who Jesus is.

Finally, there is a subjective element in discerning false teachers. God the Holy Spirit has taken up residence in every true Christian. Our resident teacher is a sound interpreter of the written Word and of the teachings of men. "You do not need anyone to teach you," John boldly declares (v. 27); the Holy Spirit will "guide you into all truth" (John 16:13).

This whole passage is a great corrective for our own day. Are we afraid to fellowship with those who have differences with us, yet are brothers and sisters in Christ? Are we worried when small groups of believers get together to pray and study the Bible, afraid that they may go astray without the pastor there to answer every question and correct every misunderstanding? If so, we have fallen far short of the biblical confidence in the Holy Spirit's ability to teach and guard His own.

So, there are objective criteria by which to test relationship with Christ. There are also the promptings and loving guidance of that Person who has taken up permanent residence in our lives.

THE SIN QUESTION
1 John 2:28–3:10

The emphasis on looking within to find a subjective basis for confidence that we know Jesus does raise a serious question. Paul insisted that leaders be chosen whose lives demonstrated holiness. Jude has identified false teachers by their actions. Why then does John seem to retreat from a clear-cut call for active holiness? Why does he first assure us of forgiveness when we fall and then go on to reassure us that we can be sure we know Jesus by looking within to sense responsiveness and love? Doesn't what we *do* matter anymore?

John is writing to ordinary people like you and me who became Christians, looked forward to a new kind of life, then perhaps were crushed to discover that everything wasn't different after all. The promised freedom from old habits and sins didn't come.

Experiences like these are common, because the Christian life involves growth. We are born again into a new world through faith in Christ. Yet the old *kosmos* that we knew so well has patterned our personalities. The gift of new life does *not* include spiritual amnesia that wipes away old thought patterns, emotions, and responses to stimuli. All these are still there and deeply ingrained. The old *will be replaced* but gradually, through growth—and grace.

It's the "gradually" that troubles us. We want to be rid of the old immediately. We want to be all new, *now*. When we stumble and fall and then fall again, it's only natural to wonder if we've made a mistake about our relationship with God. Perhaps we are *not* born again. Perhaps our failures and stumbling into sin indicates that we only *thought* we believed.

John writes to release us from this trap. If you want to be sure you know Him, first look within. If you are responsive, even though stumbling, if you find love in your heart, you can be confident. But what about our failures and sins? "Dear children," John writes, "*continue* in him" (2:28).

How comforting! Take your place as a child. Don't expect to be mature yet. But do continue in Him. Do keep on growing. And as you mature, you *will* come to the place of victory over sins.

John says several important things about sin in this short passage.

● Through faith we are now God's children. When Jesus appears we will be completely like Him. As we keep his promise of transformation in view and fix our desire on the goal of perfection, we will grow in purity here and now (1 John 3:1-3).

● There is no compromise with the sinfulness of sin. Violating God's standard of righteousness is sin. There is no sin in God. No one living in Him keeps on sinning (3:4-6).

● Objectively we can say that one whose life is committed to habitual sin is "of the devil" rather than of God. No one "born of God will continue to sin" (3:7-10).

Reading these verses, we become aware that John is talking about the pattern of a person's life, He is not talking about isolated acts of sin but about the direction of one's journey. The question is not, "Does he sin?" but, "Does he keep on sinning?" When God's life takes root in the human personality, that "seed remains in him" (3:9); the life of God within struggles against sin, and the Spirit nudges us in a new direction.

So, over time, there *is* the objective evidence of a righteous life to match the inner witness. Over time. Not necessarily immediately, but it *will* come. John promises, "No one who is born of God will continue to sin" (3:9). It's not possible for sin to keep us in bondage because the life of God within us will overcome the evil.

GOING DEEPER

to personalize

1. Read and reread these brief paragraphs in 1 John 2:3—3:10. Underline key thoughts in your Bible.

2. How many kinds of knowing can you think of or find in a dictionary? How might each be related to religious knowledge? Which seems most important to John?

3. What **is** your reaction to the idea of inner evidences of relationship? If you look within, what do you find to give you confidence in your own relationship with God?

4. Study carefully 1 John 2:28—3:10, and see if you can list fifteen statements about sin.

5. Imagine a counseling situation in which you might go to this passage of Scripture to help another person. Write out a description of the problem the person might have, and show how this passage would help.

to probe

Does John make a distinction between sin and sins? If so, what is it? What are the implications of making or failing to make such a distinction?

2. It's all too easy to take verses out of context and read into them thoughts that are not intended. For

example, "No one who is born of God will continue to sin" (3:9) might be viewed out of context as a threat, an attack, a warning, an attempt to shame. The author suggests that in context it is a promise. What difference would it make to a reader if this phrase were taken in each of these senses? Write out your answers.

3. Research the Bible's teaching about the Holy Spirit as a teacher.

9

1 John 3:11–4:21

CALLED TO LOVE

"IT'S NOT FAIR!" Angrily he turned and hurried off to his fields. "It's always him . . . always that brother of mine!" He kicked a rock down the path.

He'd known ever since childhood that his brother was the favorite. Mom and dad hadn't ever said it right out—but he could tell. All those little smiles for his brother . . . that sickly sweet brother who never got in trouble. And those pained looks on mom's face, the lines of controlled anger on dad's, when he himself played some harmless prank. He usually tried to please them. But somehow the smiles and praise they gave him seemed grudging beside the pride that shone in their eyes when they looked at his younger brother.

They denied it, of course. More than once he lashed out angrily, "It's not fair. You love him more than me!" Then mom would put her arm around him.

"No, honey," she used to say. "You're different, you and your brother. But you're both very special to us. We do love you, son. Very much."

But all the time something deep inside him was

shouting and pounding: *I hate him! I hate him! I wish he were dead!*

And now this last insulting rejection!

Sitting there in his fields, the old hatred welled up unbearably. There was only one way. Jumping up, he searched for that jagged rock he'd kicked just a minute before. There it was! Cain picked it up and strode off to find his brother, Abel.

LOVE'S WAY
1 John 3:11-24

From the beginning God's message to man has been "Love one another" (v. 11). Yet somehow the attitude of Cain has intruded. The Old Testament commanded, "You shall love your neighbor as yourself" (Lev. 19:18). *The Dictionary of New Testament Theology* comments, "Love in this context means devotion toward one's neighbor for his sake, accepting him as a brother and letting him come into his own."[1]

Yet among the *epithumia* that move us, a spontaneous love for others is absent. We can respond affectionately and even unselfishly to those with whom we have a special tie. But even family relationships may degenerate into the anger of Cain. Hurts, frustrations, real and imagined slights, all build up. The exploding divorce rate and the deep canyons of alienation that mar so many families today are vivid evidence that the way of Cain is still with us.

The contrast is especially glaring when we see how John uses the word *love (agape)*. Love is a central reality of God's nature. "God is love," John reminds us (4:8). God expresses love in the gift of Jesus; we receive that gift by a response of love. Knowing that we are loved, and loving in return, drives out the fear that destroys trust (1 John 4:18). One who is God's and who walks in His light will necessarily live in love. Such love will not only change the character of an individual's relationship with God but also the nature of his relationships with other people. If we truly live in God, then we will live in love, for God is love.

God promises us who know Jesus that the reactions and responses of Cain will be replaced by the reactions and responses of Christ. John immediately confronts us with this contrast: "Do not be like Cain, who belonged to the evil one and murdered his brother" (3:12). Did the murder drive Cain into Satan's hands? Not at all. In fact, the murder demonstrated how deep Cain already was in the evil one's grip.

Why did Cain murder Abel? Was it due to slights or parental unfairness? No, it was "because his own actions were evil and his brother's were righteous" (3:12). Abel's good revealed Cain's sinfulness. Rather than acknowledging his sins, Cain tried to hide them from himself. He turned his shame into anger at Abel; antagonism welled up in his heart; he murdered in hatred. The entire process makes it plain that Cain did not know God.

And so we return to the theme of John's letter. How can we be confident that we know God? As we love our brothers, we can be reassured that we walk not in Cain's darkness but in Christ's light.

Contrast (1 John 3:11-16). John holds up Cain and Christ for us to compare. Cain reacts with hatred to a brother who is good. Christ responds with love to sinners who reject God. Each expresses his feelings in action. Cain takes another's life. Christ gives His own life for others. Cain's actions reveal him to be evil. Christ shows himself to be good, a God of love.

Earlier John contrasted light and darkness to help us understand the Christian life. Now he contrasts love and hatred. No one who hates lives in God. But one who lives in God will love.

Love's expression (1 John 3:16-20). John is quick to note that love is not a feeling or an intention. Love is choice that binds us to a distinctive course of action. "We ought to lay down our lives for our brothers," John says. "If anyone has material possessions and sees his brother in need but has no pity on him, how can the love of God be in him?" (3:16-17). Love is not a matter of words but of acts.

Then John adds, "This then is how we know we belong to the truth, and how we set our hearts at rest in his presence whenever our hearts condemn us" (3:19-20). John noted earlier that we may become discouraged when we find ourselves slipping, unwillingly, into sins. He encouraged us to look within. See love awakening in our responsive hearts. When you and I sense responsiveness within, we can be sure we know Him.

But what if our hearts condemn us? What if, looking within, we become aware of feelings of antagonism toward a brother? What if bitterness blocks us off

BIBLE ALIVE SERIES

from giving or receiving forgiveness? If our hearts condemn rather than justify us, then it would seem logical that we do *not* know Him.

All too often you and I are aware of failure within us that others may not see. Depression may come, and with depression everything looks black. We feel guilty and helpless. John, with his deep sensitivity to our human experience, understands and answers. When it is your heart that causes you uncertainty about your relationship with God, then look for another evidence of relationship. What evidence? Love. Not as a feeling or emotion, but love expressed "with actions and in truth" (3:18). When we choose love's way in spite of our feelings, we have evidence that we know Him.

DEALING WITH UNCERTAINTY ABOUT RELATIONSHIP WITH GOD

UNCERTAIN	CONFIDENT	UNCERTAIN
because we see ourselves slip into acts of sin.	because our hearts are responsive and we feel loving.	because we feel ourselves drawn to sin and antagonistic to our brothers.
then . . . examine heart, and sense the desire to be responsive.	*then* . . . We choose to be obedient and practice love.	*then* . . . examine actions and see obedience and love practiced.
This is evidence we know Him.	This is evidence we know Him.	This is evidence we know Him.

108

God's desire is for each of us to find rest in the chart's center column. But if we find ourselves troubled by a nagging uncertainty because of either our actions or our hearts, God wants us to continue to trust. As we live in Him, His Spirit will purify and transform us.

The joyful prospect (1 John 3:21-24). In Christ we can come to the place where we no longer condemn ourselves. We can stand before God with confidence and joy, knowing that all is at peace between Him and us because of Jesus' life within us. As we believe, obey, and love, His Spirit brings the reality of fellowship into our experience.

FALSE TEACHERS
1 John 4:1-6

John now turns to this repeated theme of the "last word" letters. How can we test for counterfeits and false prophets? First, doctrinally. Jesus, God's Son, has come in the flesh. This confession will never be made by the false prophet. And second, by life-style. The world, with its "cravings of sinful man, the lust of his eyes and his pride in possessions" (2:16), is put away by the mature believer. When a teacher speaks from the viewpoint of the world, we know he is not from God.

The true believer will also recognize John's writings as God's truth. The Holy Spirit will confirm it. When teaching is out of harmony with the written Word, the Spirit Himself will bring disquiet to the believer.

BIBLE ALIVE SERIES

DIMENSIONS OF LOVE
1 John 4:7-21

In these next verses John helps us see the way of love in the Christian community. He wants us to experience close fellowship with Jesus and the Father and live in intimate community with fellow-believers. John is not exhorting us to pump up the emotion we call love. He is explaining why love is valuable to the church and how we can choose to live love.

In these verses there is no threat to make us feel guilty if we have fallen short of love. John does not lay a burden of obligation to make us struggle harder to do something we cannot do. Instead he simply points out that God is love, and to live in fellowship with Him is to live in love. If in our association with other Christians we fall into the world's way of antagonism and selfishness, then we are not experiencing God's presence.

These words of John bring hope. If we have failed to love, we acknowledge our sin to God and experience His forgiveness and cleansing. Only if we deny the importance of love in our relationships within the church, and let barriers arise between people, have we lost our way. What do believers need to understand about love in order to experience fellowship with God? Let's trace the thought of the passage.

Love is central (1 John 4:7-8). Because God *is* love, the person who shares God's life will love. This is simply a fact, a reflection of the reality that where there is no will to love, God is absent.

Love initiates (1 John 4:9-12). John makes abstract love personal when he explains that God loved us and "sent his Son as an atoning sacrifice for our sins" (v. 10). God's action is especially striking since *we did not love* God when He gave Himself! Loving meant initiating action without immediate return (and, in the case of many whom God loves, without *any* return). Here is a model for love in the Christian community. Since God has loved us this way, we ought to love one another in the same manner.

Relationships in society are usually governed by reciprocity. I am nice to those who are nice to me. Jim invites me to lunch; I invite him in return. I borrow tools from Stan; he borrows tools from me. Even sinners, Jesus once commented, love those who love them (Matt. 5:46). But love in the Christian community is not to depend on repayment. We are to take the initiative in loving, even when the ones we reach out to do not respond.

At first this seems like a strange instruction. Won't such lovers be taken advantage of? Won't the unresponse drain the people who care? John's answer is twofold. First, the capacity to love in this way exists in every person who is born of God. Thus, it is not a few loving the rest, but it is *all of us loving one another.* Each of us has the opportunity to reach out and initiate actions that meet the deepest needs of our brothers and sisters.

Second, as we take up the joyful burden of loving others, God, whom no one has seen, becomes strangely *visible* in the Church. We see God Himself as He "lives in us and his love is made complete in us" (v. 12). As God becomes more real among us, even those who have not responded will be touched by His love.

God does live in us (1 John 4:13-16). Is such love possible? Of course! We don't rely on any capacity of our own to love our brothers. In the person of the Holy Spirit God lives in us and will love through us. We learn to share God's love in us.

Love frees us from fear (1 John 4:17-18). John has an exciting prospect for the fearful and doubting. As we see God's love taking visible shape in the community of faith, we become more confident and more like God. "In this world," John says of the believing community, "we are like Him" (v. 17). Love transforms us. We realize that God is not angry or eager to punish; love has driven out fear.

The way love drives out fear is beautiful. When Stan became a Christian, he was antagonistic, bitter, and quick to take offense at others he thought slighted him. Burdened by a poor self-image, Stan could not believe that God accepted him with all of his faults. Every time something went wrong, Stan was sure God was punishing him and cringed. Even when everything seemed to go smoothly, there was always an aching fear that kept Stan from feeling peace or satisfaction.

Then Stan became a member of a truly loving church whose members accepted him as he was. They understood his behavior, overlooked his insults, and returned only love. They invited this unpleasant young man into their homes.

Gradually Stan began to realize that these people loved him in spite of himself. He could be real with them, and they still cared! For a time Stan became worse, testing their acceptance to see if it were real. Finally he was convinced. *He was loved!* With this discovery came a great release. Through the love of his brothers and sisters in Christ, Stan experienced the reality of God's love. The message of Calvary he had accepted intellectually now released the knots of guilt and fears deep within. When Stan found a community of people who were "like God in this world," he was freed to grow into a loving person himself.

Love is our proper response to God (1 John 4:19-21). Stan was freed to love only by being loved. John points out that it is the same with all of us. We did not love God; God loved us. God reached out first. But in being loved by God, we are freed to love in return. Then we can reach out to others.

Who do we love when God's love frees us? Yes, we love God, but we also love our brother. In fact, love of God and love of His family are so inseparably linked that John flatly states, "If anyone says, 'I love God,' yet hates his brother, he is a liar" (v. 20). Love wears no blinders that cut off some while focusing on others. When love touches us, our whole personality is affected. We see God and, sensing His love, we are drawn to Him. We see people for the first time. We reach out to touch and care. Love has transformed us.

In Christ, and in His community of faith, we *will* learn to walk in love.

BIBLE ALIVE SERIES

GOING DEEPER

to personalize

1. Read 1 John 3:11—4:21 several times. Underline what is, to you, the most significant statement. Put a check beside the most puzzling statement. Circle the verse number of the most helpful statement.

2. What do you think a loving community is like? In what ways is your own church a loving church? In what ways is it not?

3. What initiative can you take to show love in your church fellowship? Plan something specific that *you* can do.

4. Stan's story (pp. 112-113) suggests one reason why people may be uncertain about God's love for them. They need first to experience His love through His people. How did the outpouring of love minister to Stan's needs? What other kinds of needs might be met by love?

to probe

Do a study of John's use of *love (agape)*. Is it really the equivalent of Paul's use of *faith (pistis)* as some suggest? Why or why not?

---

1. "Love," *Dictionary of New Testament Theology*, 3 vols. (Grand Rapids: Zondervan, 1975), 2:540.

10

1 John 5; 2, 3 John

ETERNAL LIFE

"I CAN HARDLY WAIT TO DIE so I can live."

That rather strange statement actually reflects the attitude of some misinformed Christians who view eternal life as something to be inherited after death. Such people, who look at life with despair and feel that only eternity holds hope, are likely to be jolted by John's concluding thoughts. "God *has given* us eternal life, and this life is in His Son. He who has the Son *has* life" (5:11-12), italics mine. Eternal life is ours, and we are to enjoy it *now*.

FAITH
1 John 5:1-12

The core meaning of *faith (pistis* in Greek) is a personal relationship established by trust and trustworthiness. For a Christian to say "I believe in Jesus" is not so much a statement accepting certain beliefs *about* Jesus as it is an affirmation of trust. It is a confession that the person, Jesus Christ, about whom I learn in the Bible, has become more than a historical figure to me. I have recognized Him as a real and living person and I have not drawn back in fear. Instead, I have confidently placed all I am and all I hope to be in His hands. Faith is abandoning ourselves and our efforts and resting in Jesus' promise of forgiveness and transformation.

John's special emphasis within this core of meaning is this: Jesus' claim to be true and trustworthy has been authenticated by God. Only faith will receive the testimony about Jesus. John wants us to know that faith brings life. As we respond in faith to Jesus, we become one of a great company who *have* eternal life, now.

Faith's focus (1 John 5:1-5). John makes it clear that new birth, through which we receive life from God, comes through faith in Jesus Christ alone. This first verse says literally, "Everyone believing 'Jesus is the Christ' is born of God." John goes on to point out that believing is a trust response and that there can be no relationship with God except through Jesus.

Faith's initial act of trust ushers us into a new world in which we love God and demonstrate that love by obedience. The presence of eternal life now means that we will be able to overcome problems that trouble us. We will be strengthened by the eternal life that has taken root within our personalities. The things that are impossible for us today will become possible tomorrow.

Faith's testimony (1 John 5:6-12). The meaning of verse 6 is obscure, and it is the subject of much debate. The verse identifies Jesus as "the one who came by water and blood"—not by water only. Does John mean "came into the world"? Or "came into our lives"? Or perhaps he simply means "presented Himself to us." Does the water speak of the bag of water in the mother that breaks just before the child is born? If so, John is referring to the Incarnation and has affirmed the fact that Jesus, God's Son, entered the world as a human being to live in space and time and history. His presence was verified by men and recorded for all generations to come.

Or does the water refer to Jesus' baptism by John in the Jordan River, the initiation of His public ministry?

Does blood refer to the sacrificial death through which Jesus freed us? Certainly this is the central New Testament usage of that term.

Or does John use both terms in a very specific way to echo what he wrote in his Gospel—that on Golgotha "one of the soldiers pierced Jesus' side with a spear, bringing a sudden flow of blood and water" (John 19:34)?

Whatever John may have in mind for the first two sources of testimony, he adds a third that is very clear. God the Holy Spirit gives a testimony to each believer that is in harmony with the other two. History tells us of Jesus' birth as a man. Scripture records His death and resurrection and explains the meaning of those events. As we hear the gospel story, God's own Holy Spirit confirms its truth within us. These three witnesses provide a unified testimony to Jesus that we can accept, for God's testimony is sure. When we hear and believe, we *know;* God the Spirit confirms the truth within our hearts (v. 10).

What of those who hear the Gospel promise of life and prefer to seek God in someone or something other than Jesus? John's answer is clear and unequivocal. Such a person has made God out "to be a liar, because he has not believed the testimony God has given about his Son" (v. 10). Since eternal life is only in the Son, "he who has the Son has life; he who does not have the Son of God does not have life" (v. 12).

The claim that Jesus is the only way to God angered the people of the first century. They wanted to search for God in their own ways. They wanted their philosophies, their gods and goddesses who embodied human passions and reflected the image of man. Today, too, people demand the right to do their own thing in morals and religion. They reject the idea of an absolute.

But John is not concerned with what people want to believe about God. John is concerned with *reality*. The fact is that God has spoken. *He* has said that only in Jesus can life be found. You or I may reject what He says, but our rejection will not change reality.

It's important for us to grasp the implications of the unchangeable nature of God's Word. Conferences and councils may meet and announce changes in doctrine and practice. Those who claim to represent the Church may announce that homosexuality is now acceptable, but that will not change the fact that God condemns such a life-style. Some who claim to represent the Church can announce that as we evangelize we must respect the good in other religions and not suggest that their traditional faith might not lead to God. But God says life can be found only in Jesus.

Today, as in John's day, we need to communicate to a hopeless world not the acceptable illusion people desire, but the reality they need. Jesus, God's Son, is the promise of victory—and the only way to God.

CONCLUDING REMARKS
1 John 5:13-21

John's concluding remarks summarize and apply his teachings. He helps us realize how great a gift we have received in Jesus and in each other.

Prayer (1 John 5:13-15). Our whole attitude toward prayer is changed when we know we possess eternal life now. We are not probationers, waiting uncertainly just outside the door until death ushers us into life. No, John has written so that we who believe "may know that you have eternal life" (v. 13). How does such knowledge affect our prayers? John explains that it gives us "assurance in approaching God" (v. 14).

Will God accept us? Have our failures made Him angry? Has God turned His back on us because of some inner attitude that lurks, still unchanged, in our personality? Or will He ignore us because of some habits we are not yet able to break? Such fears keep us from praying with confidence.

But John's letter has quieted these fears. There have been failures, but the blood of Christ cleanses. Sin, confessed, forgiven, and forgotten is no barrier to fellowship with God. Is an inner attitude still warped? Are aspects of my life-style still unchanged? John tells us we *have* eternal life through faith in Jesus. We will see His life in us overcome our shortcomings.

With such concerns laid to rest, what should be our major prayer concern? Only that what we ask—what we desire—be what God wants too. Whatever we ask that fits His will, we can be sure we *have*.

The word for God's will here is *thelama*. It does not usually refer to God's decree or unalterable plan, but what God desires to happen. We might say that praying in God's will means harmonizing our wishes and desires with God's.

How is such a harmony possible? First, God reveals His values, attitudes, plans, purposes, and intentions to us. We know, for instance, that the pride of possessions that motivates people of the world is rejected by God. He values persons, not things. It follows then that a request to God expressing a prideful desire for possessions is not according to His will. We can expect such a request to be refused. But we can expect a request in harmony with God's own deep concern for persons to be heard and granted. So understanding and adopting God's values helps us pray in His will.

It is also possible for us to pray according to God's will because the Holy Spirit lives within us. His voice is heard by believers. He can lead us to desire and pray for those things God wants for us.

It's important to realize that John is *not* stating a condition we must meet before we can expect God to answer prayer. Just the opposite! With our relationship to God established in Christ, we can approach God with confidence. As God the Spirit works within us, our prayers will more and more harmonize with God's will. We can look forward to answered prayer as a daily experience in our Christian life.

Sin in the fellowship (1 John 5:16-17). When we acknowledge our sins to God, He forgives and cleanses us. But what if we see a fellow Christian slip? John encourages us to pray for the brother. God will answer our prayer and bring our brother back.

John does note, however, that there "is a sin that leads to death" (5:16). Is John teaching that those who have eternal life can lose it?

In the Bible, *death* has several meanings. Physical death comes to all the living. Spiritual death, the legacy of sin, grips each of us until its hold is broken by Christ. And there is the realm of death, which is that experience of alienation from God, of captivity to the world's ways, from which the believer is rescued.

John tends to overlook physical death; to him, the glorious present possession of eternal life is so vital and real that the moment of transfer from this world to the world beyond is hardly of concern.

Yet even for the believer, sin can lead us back to experience death. What sin? Sin denied or unconfessed. Sin justified by excuse and argument. Sin not brought under the covering of Jesus' blood because we choose to turn from the light to wander in darkness. What John seems to be saying here is that there is sin that opens directly into this realm of death. Not every sin catapults us into the world of illusion from which we have been delivered. But some do.

If we see a brother whose angry spirit leads him to strike out at others or whose desires are still captivated at times by greed, we are to pray for him. Such wrongdoing is sin, but it does not necessarily blind our brother to the light.

But some sins are so dark that choosing them returns a person to the deepest darkness of this world. What are these sins? John doesn't say.

What he does say is that the one born of God *will not continue to sin*. The life of God within will struggle against sin and bring the believer again to the light. The whole world may be under the control of the evil one, but the one who has new life from God is kept safe: "the evil one does not touch him" (5:18).

While John does not define the sin that leads directly into the realms of death, it is possible to speculate. All these "last word" letters are concerned with heresy, with false teaching about doctrine and life-style. John himself has said that false teachers wormed their way into the fellowship of the church but later "went out from us, but they did not really belong to us" (1 John 2:19). It seems likely that the sin of which John is speaking is that of apostasy: of turning away from both Christian truth and life.

Wait, John is saying. If you see a brother turn

away from Christ, withhold your prayers. If the person has been born of God, he will not continue in his sin. God will protect him from Satan's grasp and bring him back. But if his departure indicates that he *is* a false brother, then he will settle down in the world of death and darkness, which is his home and his destiny.

How delicately John has put it all. For you and me, there is no question about our personal relationship with Christ. We each know our own hearts; we receive His testimony and His assurance of eternal life. But we do not judge another who claims to be a brother. We pray when we see one brother troubled by sin's remaining taint. If another turns dramatically away from Christ, we wait. If He is one of God's own, he will be kept safe and will return.

About others we withhold judgment.

About ourselves we can be sure!

2, 3 JOHN

These two brief letters to individuals show how completely the themes we've seen in John's first letter dominate his later thinking. Joy comes from walking in the truth. We are called and commanded to "live a life of love" (2 John 6). As we continue in the teaching of Christ, we are protected from the deceivers who snap and tear at Christ's Body on earth.

Through it all we share the joy and love of those who, with us, have fellowship with the Father and with His Son, Jesus Christ.

BIBLE ALIVE SERIES

GOING DEEPER

to personalize

1. Read 1 John 5 and 2 and 3 John several times.

2. John speaks of our new life in Christ as eternal life. Why might God have chosen the word *eternal*? List at least eight possible ideas suggested by *eternal*.

3. There are several passages in 1 John 5 over which scholars dispute. Look up one of them in commentaries or other resources to find possible meanings beside that which the author suggests:
- 1 John 5:6-7. Jesus came by water and blood.
- 1 John 5:14. Asking according to His will.
- 1 John 5:16-17. The sin that leads to death.

4. John's purpose in writing his first letter is that we be sure we know Jesus. Looking over the entire letter, what gives you confidence that you know Jesus and have eternal life?

5. Write a commentary on either 2 or 3 John. In your commentary (which should be about five pages long) explain the things John says by referring to teachings in his first letter.

to probe

1. Write an extensive paper on one of the three problem passages noted in *personalize* 3.

2. Do a study of John's use of *life* and *death* in all his writings.

3. Many have noted that John's language and approach is designed to combat Gnosticism. What can you find out about Gnosticism? What in John's first letter speaks directly to issues it raises?

Part Four
NEW TESTAMENT THEOLOGY REVIEW

11
Selected New Testament passages

GOD'S PERSONAL TOUCH

FROM THIS VANTAGE POINT near the end of the apostolic age, we can look back to summarize what has been revealed in the New Testament. The long, gradual unfolding of truth in the Old Testament has suddenly been expanded dramatically. How do the two synchronize?

Some contrasts between the Testaments are obvious. Revelations in the Old Testament were intimately connected with a long series of historical events, the books themselves were written over a span of a thousand years. The New Testament revelation focuses on the historical events of Jesus' incarnation, death, and resurrection, and the entire New Testament was completed within decades.

The Old Testament confirms a unique relationship between God and Israel, a nation set apart from all others by a special Covenant with Him. The New Testament establishes the New Covenant that had been promised but not fulfilled. It extends the benefits of relationship with God to all men.

The Old Testament looks forward to the coming of the Messiah. The New Testament looks back, seeing in the cross and resurrection the fulfillment of promises made to God's people. From the perspective of the cross we can understand much that was shadowy and obscure.

We can find other contrasts. Law, as a way of responding to God, has been replaced. The intimacy of the spiritual family relationship provides immediate access to God, superseding the system of sacrifice that served to demonstrate that sin still blocked us from the Holy of Holies. And the priesthood of the few, appointed to hold open the door to God, has been expanded to include all who know Him. These and many other differences between the Old and New Testaments stand out. Yet in each contrast, the unity of the two Testaments is maintained. Law was set aside, but not righteousness. An inner pathway to holiness is revealed, characterized by responsiveness to the Spirit rather than dependence on external obedience for justification. All this we've explored in earlier studies. The underlying reality that is the foundation of both Testaments has remained unchanged.

In looking at New Testament theology we are *not* looking for a different God or a different faith. Instead we look to see the specific unveilings that make the New Testament the completion, rather than the replacement, of the Old. The most significant unveilings we will find have to do with man, God, and man's relationship to God.

MAN
Hebrews 2; Romans 8:15-31

The Old Testament presents the human race as the apex of God's creation. Only we share the image of God; only we participate in dominion over creation (Gen. 1; Ps. 8). The New Testament reveals that God did not intend for us to remain creatures forever. God means to lift us to glory as sons, acknowledging us as Jesus' brothers.

Hebrews 2 establishes that we are God's special concern. We are so important to God that He chose to share our humanity and, by dying, freed us from our bondage to death. The evolutionary theory encourages us to search for our roots in the heavings of some primeval sea and to see ourselves as the product of random matchings and mutations. But the Bible affirms man's uniqueness. Our roots are in God's act of creation. We are the product of His conscious, loving plan. Each human being has worth and dignity because God affirms our identity and importance.

SIN
Romans 1:18-21; Romans 5:12-21

While we are the focus of creation and the object of God's love, we are still sinners. Genesis tells us of the entrance of sin into human history. The rest of the Old Testament traces the impact of sin on individuals and society. In spite of clear guidelines from God outlining the way of holiness, Israel constantly turned from the Law to sin and idolatry. Some terrible moral fault seems to warp and twist individuals and society.

In the New Testament Paul explains that sin makes us unresponsive to God. Rather than choosing to reach out to Him, we jerk away. We desire darkness rather than light, and willingly commit ourselves to selfishness and sin. Sin is more than lawless acts, it is woven into our fallen nature. We commit acts of sin because we are sinners: the moral distortion that brings tragedy to the race is deeply embedded in each individual's personality.

Why do people reject a God who loves them and wants only their best? Sin. For sin alienates us and expresses itself in antagonism to the true God.

Why do men and women who know what is right persist in choosing to do wrong? Sin. For sin motivates us to unreasonable passions for evil.

Why are we who share a common humanity divided into warring camps by hurts and hatreds? Sin. For sin demands that selfish passions be satisfied. Sin angrily rejects others who seem to threaten satisfaction of our selfish needs.

Why do societies develop in ways that institutionalize injustice, create poverty, and dehumanize the poor? Sin. All the alienation, all the antagonism and selfishness of individuals, is multiplied in society. Injustice is the social expression of a fault rooted deeply within the personality of every person born into our world.

Sin has not changed the fact that God loves me or that He sees I have worth and value. But sin has cut me off from the experience of God's love and has kept me from enjoying God's kind of love in human relationships.

DEATH
Ephesians 2; Romans 5:1-14

When I turn from God to sin, I cut myself off from the source of life and become subject to death. The Genesis story records how God warned Adam that the day he ate from the forbidden tree, he would die. And death came: immediate death as alienation from God and His life, followed all too soon by a physical death that separates us from the material universe as well. *The Dictionary of New Testament Theology* comments that this immediate death is the basic condition of the sinner's life. "He lives as a sinner *in* death. Death is thus the power dominating his life, and to that extent a *present* reality. 'Spiritual' death and 'physical' death, inextricably bound up together, constitute the reality of a life in sin."[1]

The fact of our death in sin explains our helplessness. Where there is no life, there can be no hope. Physical death cuts us off completely from the material universe. There is no response to sights or sounds or touch: the capacity to respond to such stimuli is gone. Just so, spiritual death cuts us off completely from God. There is no response to His words or acts or touch: the capacity to respond to Him is completely extinguished.

Our only hope lies not in any efforts we might

make to reestablish relationship with God, but in the possibility that He may act. The only act of God that can help is if He would give a gift of life. Only an inner resurrection, bringing life where there is death, can meet our need.

LIFE
John 3:16-21; Ephesians 2:1-10

The Bible says God "gives life to the dead and calls into existence the things that do not exist" (Rom. 4:17, RSV). What we could not earn or merit, God provided as a free gift. "When we were dead," the Bible says, He "made us alive with Christ" (Eph. 2:5).

As we have seen in 1 John, the life God gives us is *eternal* life. It is eternal because of its endless extent. It is eternal because it is God's own life. Peter calls the gift of life an implanting within the believer's personality of God's own imperishable seed (1 Pet. 1:23).

In the New Testament the great dividing line between people is not religious, sociological, or racial. It does not matter whether we are born into a Christian, Buddhist, or Communist culture. It does not matter whether we are rich or poor, ignorant or educated, oppressed or oppressor. The great issue is simply: do we have the life of God within, or are we still in the realm of death?

Many of our debates and differences recede to insignificance in the face of this basic question. Are your practices like mine? Do you believe the same way about prophecy? Do your ideas of holiness match mine? Does your experience of the Holy Spirit duplicate my own? Such issues divide Christians today. But in God's sight the dividing line is: Have you received new life from Christ? Then you belong to Him . . . along with all the rest of His forever family. Do you lack the new life? Then you stumble in the realm of death, cut off from the life of God, out of fellowship with Him and His people.

FAITH
Romans 4; Galatians 3

In the Old Testament, God's relationship with His people is defined by Covenant, a commitment, or promise. The Psalms are full of expressions of confidence in God's faithfulness to His Covenant promises. "I have trusted in thy steadfast love; my heart shall rejoice in thy salvation," says David (Ps. 13:5).

Such expressions focus attention on the trust relationship that developed between God and His people. Faith is not a discovery of the New Testament writers. It is the eternal bridge of relationship spanning the gulf caused by sin. What the New Testament does is to put that faith relationship in sharp focus and calls for individual response to God.

The New Testament points out that each individual has an opportunity to receive God's offer of salvation as a free gift. Each of us must choose to make a commitment to Jesus as Savior and Lord or to hold back. Opportunity and decision both hinge on trust. Life and death depend on our responding in faith to God's presentation of Himself in Christ as trustworthy.

In Old Testament times the individual seems almost submerged in the nation. It is Israel as a whole that is disobedient and disciplined or responsive and victorious. It is Israel that has a destiny... Messiah is to come to deliver the chosen people. Individuals were noticed and cared for by God, but the nation was the focus of the prophets' concern.

In the New Testament, however, the faith-invitation is directed to individuals, not to a nation. It is not the historic destiny of a political or religious unit that is at stake; it is the eternal destiny of each man and woman. When the New Testament speaks of faith, the doorway of invitation is opened wide and each person may choose to step across—or not.

RESURRECTION
1 Corinthians 15; 1 Thessalonians 4:13-18

In speaking of eternal life, the New Testament gives a new emphasis to resurrection. Jesus presented Himself as "the resurrection and the life" (John 11:25). Individuals can look forward to an endless life in a place prepared for them (John 14:2). What's more, the ancient and terrible grip of sin is at last to be broken. In the resurrection "we shall be like him, for we shall see him as he is" (1 John 3:2).

The Old Testament does speak of resurrection (Isa. 26:19; Dan. 12:2). But its focus is on God's purpose for mankind on earth, not on the eternal destiny of the individual. When the promised Messiah comes, God will redeem His people. He will establish justice on earth, bring the Gentiles into the Covenant of God, and reign over a Kingdom that supplants all the competing kingdoms of man. The shattering impact of war, the degradation of poverty, the pain of sickness and early death—all these will be abolished when the Messiah comes to reign.

Then comes the revelation of the New Covenant in Christ's blood. Not only will Jesus the Messiah bring in the Kingdom; Jesus the Messiah will bring individuals into eternal life *now*. He will call out men and women to live God's life in the sin-warped world. Then they will experience a personal resurrection in which they are transformed, forever to reflect Jesus in their restored personalities.

The Kingdom promises will be kept. Jesus speaks of them (Matt. 24). The early church expected them (Acts 1:3, 6-7). The whole New Testament strains forward to a second, visible coming of its Lord (1 Cor. 1:7; 1 Thess. 4:16-18). But the visible Kingdom of Jesus on earth is now understood as only one part of God's complex and wonderful plan. Individuals can look forward to resurrection and eternal life.

The New Testament even reveals a resurrection for all of creation. This universe will be dissolved in a fervent heat and put away like a worn-out garment. Then God will shape a new heaven and a new earth to be the home of righteousness (Rom. 8:18-21; 2 Pet. 3:13).

But what of those who pass from this world without faith and life? What of those who fight any response to God and choose the darkness rather than light? There is resurrection for them too, but not to life and fellowship with God. Their resurrection is to death and endless separation, which the Bible graphically calls a "lake of fire" (Rev. 20:13-15). God, unwilling that any should perish, offers the free gift to all. But not all will accept the gift.

Through both Testaments the underlying reality remains the same. God seeks personal relationship with us, whom He created in His image. *God's deep personal concern for* us is revealed through the whole of Scripture.

The teachings about man's nature, about sin, about death and life, about faith and resurrection, are to be found in the Old as well as the New Testaments. But in the New Testament the focus is sharpened. The searchlight of revelation is focused directly upon these questions. Now we can know the destiny that is ours in Jesus Christ.

GOING DEEPER

to personalize:

1. Choose two of the topic areas discussed in this chapter and read the passages. What additional insights do you personally receive?

2. Using a concordance, trace the key word of one of the topics through both Old and New Testaments. Write up your findings.

1. "Death," *Dictionary of New Testament Theology*, 3 vols. (Grand Rapids: Zondervan, 1975), 1:436.

12

selected New Testament passages

GOD STOOPS TO CARE

THE NEW TESTAMENT BRINGS our destiny in Christ into focus. The realities of God's dealings with people are fully exposed now; what was just hinted at is now given great attention. Something similar happens in relation to God Himself. We know much about God through His words and His mighty acts in the Old Testament. Yet the deepest revelation of God as a person awaited the coming of Jesus, in whom we truly come to know the God of love.

PERSONHOOD
Ephesians 1:1-14; John 17

The Old Testament begins with God. The underlying reality in Genesis 1 is not the material universe but God. He is always viewed as a person, not a mindless force. He is a person who plans, chooses, acts, and enjoys His labors.

But the person of God seems remote in much of the Old Testament. The warmth of intimate relationship, while known by many (such as the psalmists) was not central in each believer's experience of God. God was faithful, yes. He loved His people; acted for them when they were in need; disciplined them when they strayed; guided them spiritually, morally, and socially through the Law. But still there was hesitancy. The Israelites did not easily call God "Father." Abraham and Isaac and Jacob were fathers to the race.

The New Testament reveals God not only as a person but as a person desiring intimacy. The dominant image of God in the New Testament is that of Father. He has all the attributes of personhood and a warmth in His every act that, while present in the old days, was not fully understood. Paul expresses it amazingly: We now cry out to God, *"Abba,* Father" (Rom. 8:15). We feel the impact of this cry when we realize that *Abba* is one of the first words an Aramaic child uttered as he reached up toward a father who bent down to cuddle him: *Abba* is "Daddy."

God a person? Yes. And such a person: the Sovereign Lord, the Creator, the Redeemer, the King of Hosts, the Mighty God ... all this ... and to us, "Daddy."

TRINITY
John 5:16-47

There are numerous indications in the Old Testament that the one God of Israel is a unity of persons. "Let us make man in our image," God says (Gen. 1:26). Even that great statement of affirmation given Israel in Deuteronomy 6:4, "Hear, O Israel, the Lord our God is one Lord," selects as the word for *one* a term used for "a cluster of, or composed of many, grapes."

The New Testament adds to the hint of plurality by revealing the three persons who make up the Trinity. There is the Father. There is the Son. And there is the Holy Spirit. Each distinct, yet together one.

Neither the Old nor the New Testament attempts to explain how three can be one. Instead they simply insist that Father and Son are one (John 1:1; 10:30); that the Spirit proceeds from Father and Son (John 15:26); that each is a personality distinct from the other, while one with the others (Mark 1:10-11; John 14:26; 16:12-15).

This is a great mystery that no analogy can explain. No definition that leans toward modalism (the idea that the One simply expresses Himself in three aspects or modes) nor a definition that robs the Son and Spirit of their deity will do. Trinity is an unavoidable truth in the New Testament. Understanding that mystery awaits our resurrection.

INCARNATION
John 1:1-5; Philippians 2:1-11

Old Testament history provides many evidences of God's concern for His people. But the ultimate evidence of God's willingness to become involved in our human condition is the Incarnation. In wonder Paul repeats a confession of faith of the early church:

> He appeared in a body,
>   was vindicated by the Spirit,
> was seen by angels,
>   was preached among the nations,
> was believed on in the world,
>   was taken up in glory.
>
> *1 Timothy 3:16*

Jesus often spoke of His coming from the Father and returning to the Father. The clear teaching of the New Testament is that the Son existed as God from all eternity with the Father. In an inconceivable act of self-emptying, the eternal Son set aside His prerogative as God and entered the world He had created... as a baby. Hebrews 2:14 puts it, "He too shared in their humanity so that by his death he might destroy him who holds the power of death." To accomplish His redemptive work, God became fully man, blending into one the divine and human natures.

It's clear from Scripture that there is distinctive purpose behind the Incarnation. The central goal was to accomplish redemption: Jesus lived a sinless life and died a sacrificial death in atonement for our sins. Yet there were other purposes as well. For the first time, God was *seen* in our world. Jesus' life and actions expresses the person of God in ways no words could have. His life defines holiness. His compassion explains love. His patience opens our eyes to God's heart attitude toward you and me. Most of all the Incarnation tells us that God cares enough to become involved. He does not stand back, urging us on from a safe vantage point. He strips Himself of His glory and, accepting the form of a man, humbles Himself even to death.

Once and for all the Incarnation decides the unsettling question, "What does God really think about me?" Is God a policeman, looking for crimes to punish? Or a nagging parent, always finding fault? Is He an impersonal force, oblivious to insignificant humans He crushes beneath the steamroller of history? Is God an idealist, who in His concern to restructure society ignores the individual? Or is He so caught up in Himself that He demands we cringe before Him, caring only that we offer fearful praise? What *does* God think of us?

To Him we are not criminals, not naughty children, not ants, not pawns in some grand plan, not nothings. To God we are special, the objects of His love and concern. Rather than demanding service from us, He sets aside His robes of glory and becomes our Servant. Rather than demand full payment from us for sin, He gives His own life in our place. He became man to tell us He loves us.

SACRIFICE
Hebrews 10; Romans 3:21-16

The death of the incarnate Christ on Calvary was

the climax of His life on earth; it was an event exceeded in significance only by the resurrection. The New Testament explains that death as an atoning sacrifice.

In the Old Testament sacrifice played a central role in Israel's spiritual experience. Immediately after He gave the Law, God instituted the sacrificial system. The blood of the sacrificial animal, offered on the altar, made atonement, or covering, for sin. Sin was not removed, but it was covered. God was then free to act in grace toward those He loved even though their characters and actions cried out for judgment. The question "How can a holy God deal kindly with sinful man?" is answered in the Old Testament by sacrifice. "I have given [the blood] . . . upon the altar to make atonement for your souls" (Lev. 17:11).

But the blood of sacrificial animals was not able to remove sin, only cover it. Death is the necessary and essential outcome of sin. Paul explains, "The wages of sin is death" (Rom. 6:23). Even God could not set aside this necessity: between darkness and light, holiness and sin, death and life, there can be no compromise. The issue must be faced and resolved.

The New Testament reveals the divine solution. Sin brings death, but God sent His own Son to die as a substitute for the sinner. God presented Jesus, the Bible says,

> as a sacrifice of atonement, through faith in his blood. He did this to demonstrate his justice, because in his forbearance he had left the sins com-

mitted beforehand unpunished—he did it to demonstrate his justice at the present time, so as to be just and the one who justifies the man who has faith in Jesus.
Romans 3:25-26

Hebrews explains that Jesus, by His death, entered the presence of God "once for all by his own blood, having obtained eternal redemption" for us (9:12).

The Old Testament sacrifices were, in effect, a dramatization of Calvary. The repeated lessons, teaching that only death could provide a remedy for sin, looked forward to that once-for-all death of God's Son.

And so our understanding of God grows. Who is He? A person. One in three. One who through human birth became totally involved in our condition. One who ultimately sacrificed His own life that through His death you and I might be made alive.

INDWELLING
John 14:16-27; Romans 8:1-17

God's involvement in our lives is not limited to history. Jesus entered time and space to break the power of sin and make eternal life available to us. But the New Testament reveals that God continues to be involved; the Holy Spirit lives in the renewed personality of the one who chooses to trust in Jesus.

This is one of the great contrasts between the Old and New Testaments. God always has yearned for an intimate relationship with His straying creatures. Through the Law He pointed out the way of holiness and He held the door open through sacrifice. Yet the relationship was never as close as it might have been. Those who believed trusted, accepted, and responded to the mediating Word of the Law. But there was not the *immediate* relationship, the intimacy of children and Father.

In the guidance pattern of the Old Testament, the Law was an *external* guide to holy living. It was outside the person, pointing the way for faith and standing as a testimony against unbelief. Where there was failure, sacrifice was available to restore fellowship. Yet in Old Testament times there was a veil hung between the Holy of Holies, that place in the Temple where God's presence dwelt, and the worshipers outside.

When Jesus died, the veil was torn from top to bottom to signify that the way into the Holiest is now open. Both the Law and worship revealed God's desire to have fellowship with man. Yet both also spoke of a barrier that held God back from the depth of intimacy He desired. After Jesus' resurrection God acted to initiate a close relationship. God the Holy Spirit came to take up residence within the personality of each believer.

The presence of the Holy Spirit within us is the basis for a change both in the Law and in worship. Paul says the Law was in force "until faith should be revealed" (Gal. 3:23). Now that Christ has died, responsiveness to the Spirit within replaces the external rule of the Law. The Old Testament foretold this change. Looking forward to a time when a New Covenant would replace the Mosaic, Jeremiah spoke God's promise: "I will put my law within them, and I will write it upon their hearts" (Jer. 31:33). The pathway of righteousness that the Law described is now, in the person of the Holy Spirit, engraved *within* us. God's own love of righteousness grows within us as we come to know Him better and learn to follow the leading of His Spirit within.

There is a similar change in access to God: "Let us then approach the throne of grace with confidence" (Hebrews 4:16). Paul explains that we have now received the full right of sons through faith in Jesus. "Because you are sons, God sent the Spirit of his Son into our hearts" (Gal. 4:6). As a member of the family, we have immediate access, guaranteed by the presence of the Holy Spirit in our lives.

God's involvement with individuals, even the unthinkably *total* involvement of God in each believer's daily life, is hinted at in the Old Testament. But the fulness of that reality is revealed only in the New.

Many Christians fail to grasp God's total involvement with us. But what a vital reality to see! *We are never alone; we are never cut off from God's presence.* In every time of need, whether for mercy (because we have failed), or for grace to help (when we are challenged beyond our ability), we have the fullness of God Himself within. In the person of the Holy Spirit, God continues to reach gently into our lives. Paul, caught by the wonder of it all, praises God:

> Now to him who is able to do immeasurably more than all we ask or imagine, according to his power that is at work within us, to him be glory in the church and in Christ Jesus throughout all generations, forever and ever!
>
> Amen.
> *Ephesians 3:20-21*

New Testament theology sharpens the Old Testament's portrait of man and God. The New Testament does not change God's attributes or character, but it does give fresh definition and emphasis to certain qualities. It was possible to speak of God as a Father before Jesus entered the world. But until Jesus expressed the love of God, we could never call Him "Daddy." The depth of God's commitment to us was unmistakably revealed in the Incarnation. Today, warmly linked to God by His Holy Spirit, we know Him in a personal, intimate way. For our God has bent down to earth, touched our lives, and let us know how much He cares.

GOING DEEPER

to personalize

1. Which dimension of God's New Testament revelation of Himself seems hardest for people to grasp? Why do you think this is so?

2. Read the passages listed for two of the topics.

3. Explore one of the topics with a concordance. Find out all you can about it and write up your

findings in a two- to four-page report.

to probe

1. Discover what the Old Testament reveals about one of the topics. What could have been known by Old Testament believers? What information awaited the fuller revelation of the New?

2. How does the Holy Spirit replace law as the guiding force in the believer's life? Report in a five- to-seven page paper what the New Testament says about this theme.

13
selected passages

GOD AND HIS FAMILY

IT'S CLEAR FROM OUR LOOK at New Testament theology that New Testament revelation is distinctively relational; it focuses on persons, especially on the relationship between God and man.

But the message of the New Testament depicts not only the vertical relationship of the individual and God, but also the horizontal relationship of one individual with another. In special focus are relationships within the church. Ephesians 3:14 speaks of God the Father as the one "from whom the whole family of believers" derives its name. What is our name, and how do we derive it from Him? Our name is *family,* and we derive it from God's essential nature as Father. Clearly all those who are children of the Father must be brothers and sisters to one another. And so we have a new insight into relationships within the community of faith. The Old Testament called on the Israelite to love his neighbor as himself (Lev. 19:18). The New Testament calls on

Christians to love one another as Christ has loved us (John 13: 34-35). That's what it means to be in God's family.

NEW BIRTH
John 3

Entering into a new spiritual life is like being born again. The analogy has many implications. One is closely associated with growth. A newborn child has the potential for maturity; yet the fulfillment of that potential comes only after a long process of growth and learning. The Christian too is urged to keep on growing in Him and is reminded that we "are being built together" to become a dwelling in which God lives by His Spirit (Eph. 2: 22).

There is another implication that is sometimes overlooked. Birth catapults the newborn into a different world in which a total life-style must be learned. Understandings, attitudes, values, and behaviors must be developed.

Spiritual birth may come after understandings, attitudes, values, and behaviors that contradict the Christian life-style have been deeply ingrained. Colossians says that God has "rescued us from the dominion of darkness and brought us into the kingdom of the Son he loves" (1: 13). A citizen of God's kingdom has to reject the old ways of darkness while learning how to live a new life.

This kind of learning involves far more than gaining new information: a personality is being rebuilt. To understand how spiritual growth takes place, we need only look at the process of an infant growing. How does a maturing child learn to function in society? Essentially, life-style is learned and personality shaped in the family. In the context of intimate and loving relationships provided by the family, a way of life is both taught and caught, explained and modeled. The family relationship provides the essential context for the growth of an infant. In the same way, every born-again Christian needs a family in which to grow.

The exciting announcement of the New Testament is that God has provided just such a family for us in one another!

ONE FAMILY
Ephesians 2:11–3:20; Romans 12

Three New Testament figures portray the community of those who have been given life in Christ. One is family. This is reflected in the New Testament's many uses of the terms *brother* and *sister* and in multiple references to our new position as children of God. The second figure is that of a body. We are pictured in such intimate relationship with Jesus and one another that only the organic relationship of cell linked to cell, interdependent organs, and a head in loving control, can portray the reality. The third picture is of a temple into which both individuals and the church as a whole built as a fitting home for God's Holy Spirit.

In each of these figures, intimate relationship, oneness, and unity are stressed. We are linked to one another as brothers and sisters, fitted together as parts of the body, joined by the Master Builder so no cracks appear between the building blocks. The family analogy stresses the quality of relationship, the body highlights the division of labor, and the temple portrays essential holiness.

But why was the family chosen to epitomize a quality relationship? And what characteristics of family relationships are most significant?

If it is going to be normal and healthy, a family needs to express love and acceptance. The family expresses attitudes and values in daily behavior and explores these in conversation. So a healthy family life is marked by open communication, by honest sharing of what is happening within each person. The family is a shared life, with example and instruction, correction and encouragement. There life-style and character develop.

How striking then to see these same characteristics in the New Testament church. "Be devoted to one another in brotherly love," Paul says (Rom. 12:10). Christians are called to long-term commitment, shared lives, and open communication. We are to live comfortably with others and look to our leaders for an example of the kind of persons we are to become.

God has provided believers with a family in which He means for us to live and grow.

At times we lose this vision of the church as a family, and we think of it as an organization. We think of it as buildings and programs and activities, rather than as a network of relationships. We involve ourselves with tasks, committees, and service at the expense of love for one another. We neglect getting to know and supporting each other. It's then that our growth in Christ is stunted or warped. Just as poor family relationships cause personality problems for growing children, poor relationships within the family of God cause problems for growing Christians. But poor relationships are not necessary! We can recover the New Testament emphasis on the church as family . . . and love one another as Christ commands.

TRANSFORMATION
Romans 8:28-29; 2 Corinthians 3; 1 Corinthians 13

What kind of growth can be expected in the newborn Christian? The Bible says we shall take on Jesus' likeness. "We shall be like him," John promises, "for we shall see him as he is" (1 John 3:2).

This transformation does not imply loss of individual personality or identity. It does mean, however, a change in values and perspectives, a new love for light, and a rejection of darkness. It means we will love God and will want to take on His motivations and desires.

In our last chapter we saw that the New Testament brings God's love into clear focus. As we are transformed, we will grow to love "as I have loved you" (John 13:34). "Love your enemies," Jesus instructed His disciples (Matt. 5:43). He went on to demonstrate that kind of love by dying for those who were so eager to kill Him.

It's helpful to think of transformation as becoming loving. Paul says, "your attitude should be the same as that of Christ Jesus" (Phil. 2:5). He then goes on to portray the love expressed by Jesus as He became a servant and then died for us. What's more, the New Testament gives an interesting equation linking love and law. "He who loves his fellow man," Paul says, "has fulfilled the law." All the commandments are "summed up in this one rule: 'Love your neighbor as yourself.' Love does no harm to its neighbor. Therefore love is the fulfillment of law" (Rom. 13:8-10).

INCARNATION
Ephesians 4:17–5:20; Colossians 2:6-15; 3:1-17

When John writes, "Whoever claims to live in him must walk as Jesus did" (1 John 2:6), he introduces an amazing truth. *The Incarnation is not ended!*

Jesus perfectly expressed the reality of God in a human personality. We can never enflesh God as He did, in fullness. But we *do* express God in this world. God has taken up residence in us and through the Word and the Spirit and the family is reshaping us to be like Jesus. Paul bluntly says that we "reflect the Lord's glory," for we "are being transformed into his likeness with ever-increasing glory, which comes from the Lord, who is the Spirit" (2 Cor. 3:18). God still walks the earth in the person of the believer. He still expresses His love through incarnation.

We can see why the family is so vital in God's plan and why the church as a family receives so much

New Testament attention. It is in the family that the newborn are nurtured. It is in the family that transformation takes place. If we are to represent God in our world today, we must be like Jesus. If we are to become like Jesus, the church must be the family God designed . . . not an impersonal organization.

What happens as we incarnate God? First, as we live a life of love, we help everyone see God as the loving Father He is. Secondly, as we live a holy life, we turn our backs on the sins that destroy individuals and society. Our full commitment to God's values and priorities is a vivid testimony to God. Jesus, the light of the world, is reflected in our faces. In that reflection both evil and good are made known to all people.

A third aspect of incarnation is seen in the direction of our love. It is intense for those who are our brothers and sisters, but it is also warm for those who are as yet outside the family. We can express our love in concern for physical and social as well as spiritual needs of those around us. Jesus fed the hungry crowds and healed the paralytic as well as forgave him.

At the same time, the Christian's concern must be for people's deepest need, for release from sin's grip. Jesus sought out sinners, explaining that the sick, not the healthy, need a doctor (Matt. 9:12). As we grow to be more like Jesus, we too will reach out to heal and to "seek and to save" those who are lost (Matt. 19:10).

Incarnation means that as we experience the new life, we will love our brothers and sisters, grow in holiness, and reach out to those yet living in the realm of spiritual death. Our relationships with other Christians as well as with non-Christians around us will be transformed.

And so we are again confronted with the fact that the New Testament emphasizes relationships. In the New Testament focus on persons, we are called to new ways of living, new kinds of relationships.

- With God, we are to joyfully cast off our fears and relax in the reality of a Father's love. We need never question His commitment to us.
- With fellow Christians, we are to draw closer in love and service. We are never again alone because we are members of a family that is one in Christ.
- With non-Christians, we are also to build bridges of love. We may reject their life-styles, but we are to care for the persons themselves with a respect and a compassion that reflects Christ's self-sacrificial love.

The transformation we seek will reorder our priorities. The world, with its cravings of the flesh, its lust of eye and pride in possession, will no longer appeal. Persons, not things, will become of ultimate value. And we will experience this transformation as we live together in the family of God.

GOING DEEPER

to personalize

1. How important have other Christians been in your own life? Have you experienced a close family relationship with other believers?

BIBLE ALIVE SERIES

2. Read the key passages suggested for two of these topics. Jot down any insights you gain.

3. Select one of the topics and trace it through the New Testament. What can you find that supplements the author's discussion?

4. Which of the topics do you think is most important for Christians today to understand? Why?

5. Why do you think Christians sometimes fall into the trap of viewing the church as a program, building, or organization rather than people in relationship? What could be done by an individual to help others experience the family?

to probe

Develop at least fifty test items that you believe reflect the basic teachings of all the "last word" letters.

THE NEW TESTAMENT BOOKS

DECADE	WRITING	DATE	PLACE
A.D. 40-50	James	45-46	Jerusalem
	Galatians	48	Antioch
A.D. 50-60	I Thessalonians	51	Corinth
	II Thessalonians	52	Corinth
	I Corinthians	55	Ephesus
	II Corinthians	56	Macedonia
	Romans	58	Corinth
A.D. 60-70	Matthew	60-70(?)	Antioch
	Ephesians	60-61	Rome
	Colossians	60-61	Rome
	Philemon	60-61	Rome
	Philippians	60-61	Rome
	Luke-Acts	60-70	?
	I Peter	64-65	?
	Mark	65-68(?)	Rome
	II Peter	66	?
	I Timothy	65-66	Macedonia
	Titus	65-66	Ephesus
	II Timothy	67	Rome
	Jude	67-68	Jerusalem (?)
	Hebrews	67-68	?
A.D. 70-80			
A.D. 80-90	John	85(?)	Ephesus
A.D. 90-100	I John	90-95	Ephesus
	II John	90-95	Ephesus
	III John	90-95	Ephesus
	Revelation	95-98	Patmos

Leader Supplement

PASS IT ON

INTRODUCTION

PASS IT ON surveys the Books of 1, 2 Timothy, Titus, 2 Peter, 1, 2, 3 John, and Jude. It is part of a series of twelve that constitute **Bible Alive,** a study guide for the entire Bible. Like the others, it is designed for a single purpose: to help believers come to know the Word of God and to discover God's personal message to them.

Understanding this purpose for survey helps us define our teaching goals.

THE NATURE OF BIBLE SURVEY

BIBLE SURVEY IS NOT BIBLE INTRODUCTION, which tends to focus on details *about* the Bible. Introduction courses explore such issues as authorship and canonicity. They struggle with dating and argue for or against such things as documentary hypotheses or the authorship of a book. While these issues are significant, Bible survey is not primarily concerned with them.

Nor is Bible survey concerned with apologetics—that is, the defense of some view of Scripture or the resolving of historical or philosophical problems. Again, such a discipline is significant. But it, too, tends to talk *about* the Bible—to spend time comparing Bible documents with similar material from other cultures, etc. Apologetics has a place, but not in survey.

Nor is Bible survey a series of sermons. While we want some application in any study of the Bible, survey goes beyond the exposition of application.

Survey focuses on *mastery of the Scripture itself*. We seek to grasp the content of God's Word and to discover its message for us.

In the most significant sense, Bible survey brings us to a study of Scripture. *Our concern is not what men may say about the Bible, but what the Bible says.* It is the text itself—what God is saying to us—that we are eager to master.

It may be interesting to debate evidence to show that Jonah could have been swallowed by the "great fish" or to explore the chain of internal and external evidence that leads us to place Habakkuk's book at a particular date. But such argument is set aside in Bible survey. We concentrate on the teachings and message of each Bible passage. Our goal is that our students know what God is saying in each major section of the Bible and hear what He is saying to *them* today. While survey sketches a historical context that other disciplines have defined and draws on other kinds of theological study, survey accepts the benefits of such studies and does not try to reproduce the reasonings.

What are the advantages of a survey approach?

• *We give students a foundation for lifelong Bible study.* Survey provides initial acquaintance with the whole Bible, motivating and encouraging in-depth study to follow.

• *We give an orientation to Scripture's sweep and scope.* Too many believers today are biblically ignorant. They do not know how the Bible fits together; they do not know its major themes and emphases. Our survey approach "puts the Bible together."

- *We place vital tools in believers' hands.* Someone who knows how the Bible fits together is able to interpret it more accurately than a person who grasps at a verse here or there without knowing the historical setting or the purpose of God when that passage was first written. When we understand what God's Word meant to the men and women to whom it was spoken, we can apply it in our day with much greater confidence and accuracy.

Each of these benefits can be ours when we come to the Word of God with a desire to master its content and to listen to its message. And each of them *will* be ours as we work through this portion of the New Testament. In these studies you will relate people, events, and revealed truths, tracing the progress of God's continuing revelation. And you will help each of your students hear God's Word to him or her personally. Your students will develop an appreciation for the major themes of each New Testament book and an understanding of their relevance and meaning for us today. Most important, they will meet God in His Word. For God does speak in our day. In our Bible survey studies of the text of Scripture itself, we will hear God's voice and be drawn into a closer relationship with Him.

APPROACHES TO SURVEY

THERE ARE SEVERAL WAYS to approach Bible survey. One way is thematic: taking a topic like the Law and tracing it through the Old and New Testaments, then moving on to another topic to do the same. A second approach is to focus on groupings of books, such as the Pentateuch or the poetic books. Another is dispensational: to look at different periods of time when God seems to be dealing with men in certain ways that differ from His dealings in other periods (for instance, Adam, like believers today, was not under the Law. He had no Ten Commandments to live by).

Our approach in this series is different from each of these. It is based on the *flow of history*. This is important for several reasons. First, God's revelation took place gradually. In the Old Testament period, revelation took place over many centuries of time; in the New Testament period, over decades. In each case there was a *progressive* dimension to revelation—truths were unfolded when needed by God's people, in a distinct sequence. We want to trace the unfolding of God's plan and purposes as this unfolding happens; we want to understand the Bible's teachings and events in their developmental sequence.

Second, God's revelation focused on contemporary needs. God spoke to living generations of believers, communicating the message they needed *then*. When we understand the crises which stimulated the communication of particular truths, and the historical setting into which the revelation came, we have important insights into the meaning of the written Word for us in our day.

Third, the books of the Old and New Testaments do not appear in our Bibles in the sequence in which they were written. We need to place them in order and to see the process of history if we are to fully understand God's Word.

For these major reasons our approach in our survey studies is to explore God's Book in a sequence determined by Bible history. We trace the early development of the Church across the decades after Jesus' Resurrection and look at the New Testament documents associated with them. We see the emerging Church face problems growing out of its life together and, by tracing the answers which God provided, we find answers to our problems today.

Dating. Dating and sequencing of the New Testament books and historical events are drawn primarily from Merrill C. Tenney's *New Testament Survey* and *New Testament Times.* If you wish to explore reasons behind dates given, refer to his careful documentation and reasoning.

TEACHING BIBLE SURVEY

YOUR GOAL IN TEACHING SURVEY is to involve your students in a direct exploration of the Bible and its message. You want them to interact with Scripture, not just to read the text or listen to lectures.

Teaching survey means motivating and guiding a class to dig into the Word of God, to explore together what it says and what it means.

How do the resources provided in this series help?

The Bible. Most of your students' reading will be done in Scripture. Help them select a good modern version—one that will not confuse or cloud the meaning by use of archaic English. This study is based on the *New International Version*. You may want one of the modern paraphrases (such as the *Living Bible*), or you may want a good translation (such as the *New American Standard Bible* or the *Revised Standard Version*). Encourage all your class members to use the same version, but invite them to check others when questions of interpretation arise. Most of your in-class discussion will focus on the text and on discoveries your students have made in reading God's Word.

The textbook. This book, like each of the **Bible Alive** survey texts, is designed to lead your students into direct Bible study. Each chapter of the text organizes a segment of Scripture in a way that will help your students fit that section together and sensitize them to its main message.

Thus the **Bible Alive** texts are not commentaries designed to "cover" the Bible. Instead, each is written to orient the reader to a Bible section and to encourage him to move into the Word to make his own personal discoveries within the framework provided.

Often, when large sections of the Bible are being discussed in a chapter, students will be asked to read only parts of that section in their Bibles. These are either *representative passages* (enabling them to sample a larger segment) or are *significant passages* (in which critical teachings or revelation is given). By using the textbooks to orient the reader to the scope and general meaning of a section of Scripture and

USE OF RESOURCES

The Bible: • the primary textbook; most time is to be spent in direct Bible study

The text: • gives a framework for direct Bible study

• guides the student to explore representative or significant passages

• suggests assignments for personal Bible study

The class: • helps students share discoveries

• allows learning activities to stimulate understanding and application of Bible portions read

• lets teacher add significant input, clarify, guide

Teacher supplement: • suggests teaching goals for each session

• suggests teaching methods for each class session

• gives sample quizzes and exams

then focusing attention for more intensive study of a representative or significant part of that section, you encourage maximum use of study time.

Assignments. Most chapters in the text suggest two kinds of assignment. The first type involves reading and thinking that *personalize* the message of Scripture. These assignments are designed to help the learner meet God as He speaks through His Word today. Whether your students are members of a weekly Sunday school class or are in a course given for credit in school, you'll want to take time to work through these personalized studies.

Additional assignment suggestions are given with each chapter to help the student taking a credit course. These *probe* beyond what might be expected in a less academic setting. As a teacher, you may, of course, give any or all these activities as assignments, select just a few, or develop comparable assignments of your own. It is important, however, in the credit course as well as the Sunday school or home study class, to make sure that your students examine the Scriptures for growth and enrichment and share what God is saying to them with each other.

The class itself. Your time together in class is extremely significant because through discussion and various teaching approaches you can help your class think deeply about what they have studied in Scripture and about God's message for them today.

This is also a place, of course, for lecture and input of your own ideas and research. The lesson plans provided here suggest appropriate topics and resources for short lectures; you'll have material of your own that you will feel is important as well. But in my own teaching of survey on a graduate level, I found that helping the truths of the Word come alive to my students was the most vital part of the course. The lesson plans emphasize some of the methods I used then as well as lectures (which are now, in large part, found as content in the chapters of the text).

TESTING

QUIZZES AND EXAMS are an important part of this course, but not as a basis for grading. Instead, they have value as an element in the learning process.

Good quizzes can help a student see just how much he has learned. They can motivate further study. Poor quizzes and exams are often designed to find out what the student does *not* know and to penalize him for his lack.

What is vital to realize is that the only truly significant test of success in Bible teaching is the learner's response to God and His Word long after he or she has left your class. Bible survey is designed to motivate further Bible study. Class time should help your students enter into a richer experience of all God has for them. If, as you study together, your students begin to respond more fully to God as He speaks to them, then you have real evidence of success. The ability to pass an examination is evidence neither of your success as a teacher or a student's success as a learner.

For this reason, quizzes and tests in this course are designed to give positive evidence to students of their own learning—to motivate and encourage rather than to evaluate them—and to focus students' attention on what is important for them to master.

Misuses of testing. At times, testing is used for other purposes. Sometimes tests are designed to show up what the student does not know. The almost-impossible-to-pass test that most of us have experienced does not help the teacher or the student.

At other times, tests are used primarily to encourage competition. Grading is based entirely on test performance, and so individuals view a test as a contest and view others as rivals against whom they compete. Whatever may be said for such a philosophy in secular subjects, it is a very bad dimension to build into a Christian learning experience. To grow spiritually, we need to learn how to minister to and cooperate with each other, not to compete. When testing is misunderstood or misused, its potential benefits will be lost.

Weakness of some testing. There are other ways to lose the benefits of testing. Sometimes, tests focus on facts and content to the exclusion of meaning and so only indicate the ability of individuals to memorize.

When we are dealing with Scripture, we want to stress the importance of meaning and application. Bible facts are true, yes; but they are also meaningful. God speaks to us in history and in His revealed Word in order that we might know Him and that our total personalities might be transformed. Thus factual tests have a very limited value. Our students must know the facts, but they also must know the message communicated through those facts and be aware of the need for personal response.

Appropriate testing in Christian education probes the attitudes, values, and behaviors of our students as well as their possession of information.

We can, in fact, sum up good testing by saying that it provides positive feedback to the student and teacher by giving evidence that growth is taking place in the learner across his whole personality.

My concern for developing a family feeling in class and for keeping the emphasis on the real concern of Bible teaching/learning led me to adopt an approach through which I could assign grades while removing competitiveness and intellectualism. It's called the contract system; you may wish to explore its possibilities if you are teaching in a setting where grades are to be assigned.

This approach features the following:

1. Each student is expected to be in class and to complete daily assignments.

2. Each student is to take and pass all quizzes and exams with a minimum score of 75 percent. Those who do not reach this minimum score take the test over until they do. This is called *reaching a content competency level.*

3. Students who successfully complete the first two requirements are guaranteed a C for the course. Students who wish a higher grade can earn one by taking on additional credit work. For instance:

   a. For a B, a student might complete tests and quizzes with a minimum of 80 percent and do any five extra *probe* assignments.

   b. For an A, a student might complete tests and quizzes with a minimum score of 85 percent and do ten extra *probe* assignments.

The extra assignments can be worked out between the teacher and students and should, of course, be completed satisfactorily. Or, other special projects can be assigned for extra credit, such as undertaking to teach another person what the student is learning and keeping a diary on each time the two meet, or keeping a journal in which personal thoughts, applications, and experiences are recorded.

Within this kind of framework, maximum freedom is given to individuals to explore their own interests, and grades are agreed on before the class starts. Thus, competitiveness is reduced and personal motivation is substituted for external motivations.

Finally, the contract system lets you work with your students to help them select projects which will focus on the attitudes, values, and behaviors which God seeks to touch as we come to know and hear His voice.

If you choose to adopt a contract approach for grading this study, announce it at the beginning and explore various options for special projects with your class.

The models of possible test approaches that follow are designed to help you construct tests for this series of studies that will help your students realize, "I'm growing!"

TEST MODELS

Our goal in testing is to give feedback to both teacher and student on the learner's growth and understanding in two areas. We want to know how much the student knows and understands (cognitive domain), and we want to know how his or her attitudes and values have been affected by the material (affective domain). Let's look at sample test items we can use to measure growth in each domain.

Cognitive domain. Content mastery is important in all learning. Tests here can range in scope from those that probe a student's ability to recognize, recall, and select from lists to the ability to relate, restate and integrate.

Here are several models for constructing tests of content knowledge:

- True/False.

1. *1 John and Timothy cover the same basic content.*   T   F
2. *Titus is known as "the disciple Jesus loved."*   T   F

- Completion.

1. *The letters to Timothy and Titus are known as the _____ Epistles.*
2. *Leaders of local congregations are known as _____ .*

- Recall.

1. *List three characteristics of false teachers.*
2. *Name two of the three New Testament letters that focus on how to deal with false teachers.*
3. *List at least five qualifications for spiritual leadership a church elder needs to have.*

- Multiple choice.

In the space at the left write the letter of the phrase that best completes the sentence.
1. *John's first letter deals primarily with*
   a) *how a person can know he is really a Christian.*

b) how a Christian can know he is in fellowship with God.
c) the importance of confessing sin.
d) how to distinguish true believers from counterfeit.

• *With your Bible open, construct a chart showing at least seven parallels between topics in 1 and 2 Timothy.*

Each of these approaches tests for knowledge or possession of information. It is also important to test the student's ability to use that knowledge—a significantly higher level of mastery. Here are several more demanding test types.

• *Write a commentary on 2 Peter 3. Considering the theme of Peter's letter, why did he include this section?*

• *With your Bible open, discuss heresy. Define the term, state the attitude of the "last word" letters to it, show how heretical teachers can be recognized, and describe what our response ought to be to it. Refer specifically to relevant passages.*

• *Give illustrations of how the leadership principles in the Pastorals could be applied today*
1) in selecting leaders,
2) in training leaders for their responsibilities, and
3) in guiding the direction of a local congregation.

An excellent book, *Taxonomy of Education Objectives: Handbook I: Cognitive Domain*, by Bloom, et al. (New York: David McKay), gives many additional illustrations of test types.

Affective Domain. There is another book that

thoroughly explores how to test the affective domain. I suggest you explore this important resource: *Taxonomy of Education Objectives: Handbook II, Affective Domain* by Krathwohl, et al. (New York: David McKay). Among the test types this book suggests are several easily adaptable to self-report examinations; they allow the learners to express personal comments and commitments. For example:

• *Select one trait of leaders given in these New Testament books that seem particularly important to you. Write a brief explanation of why it is important, and share how you see this trait developing in your own life.*

• *Describe the person most likely to have the greatest spiritual impact on others. Illustrate how his character traits find expression in his relationship with others.*

• *Using the spiritual criteria you established in the last question, rate yourself in each trait as*
  –definitely need change here,
  –I am encouraged by my growth here, or
  –I really feel good about myself here.
Illustrate the reasons you have for each rating.

1
1, 2 Timothy; Titus

LAST WORDS

YOU'LL HAVE TWO GOALS in mind as you hold your first class session: 1) to establish a climate for warmth and sharing, and 2) to motivate your class members to want to study carefully these New Testament letters.

The teacher can establish a sharing atmosphere in a classroom in many ways. For instance, arranging the seating in a circle and sitting down with your students is a nonverbal way of letting them know you intend to be a learner along with them rather than an authoritarian lecturer. Encouraging participation and listening carefully are important. Sharing personal feelings and experiences of your own will also set a warm, relational tone.

These last words of Paul to Timothy and Titus are often overlooked in Bible study and preaching. Yet they are ideally suited to help the now-institutionalized church discover vital principles for a deepening relationship with God.

LAUNCHING

Select one or more of the following:

1. Ask your students to identify one positive heritage they have received from their families, and to think of one or two ways it affects their lives today. Begin this sharing time with yourself, and move around the circle, allowing each person to share.

2. Divide the class into groups of three to five persons. They are to take three minutes to list, without discussion, at least ten values they would like to pass on to the next generation. Members of the groups can share their lists with the rest of the class and discuss the reasons for their choices.

INPUT

1. If your students had their textbooks before the first meeting of the class, ask each to share what he or she found when doing *personalize* 2, p. 18.

2. You should use direct Bible study frequently in class to stimulate study. Ask each person to read one chapter from either 1 or 2 Timothy, underlining any verses that seem to indicate a value, attitude, or way of living that the apostle Paul wishes to pass on to his next generation.

After five or six minutes, let the class members share their discoveries.

3. You may find it appropriate to give a brief historical overview, supplementing the notes in the textbook chapter. But do try to keep this sketch limited to five or six minutes.

BIBLE ALIVE SERIES

IMPACT

List on the chalkboard the following questions:
- What dangers lie ahead?
- How can Christianity survive persecution?
- What makes Christian experience vital today?
- How can I pass on my faith to my children?
- How do we deal with false teaching?

Ask your class to suggest other questions that might be of concern to Christians looking ahead to an uncertain future. When the list is completed, point out that these Epistles were written to answer just such questions.

Close with a time of silent prayer in which each student asks God for wisdom and direction in an area of concern suggested by one of these questions.

ASSIGNMENT: Text chapter 2; selected *Going Deeper* items.

2

1, 2 Timothy; Titus

TO TEACH OTHERS

THIS SESSION is designed to clarify the biblical concepts of teaching and learning as found in the Pastorals. It is important that we correct the narrow twentieth-century notion that teaching is simply transmitting information. We must understand the biblical stress on the communication of both truth and life-style. You should encourage your students to apply these notions to their local congregation.

LAUNCHING

Select one or more of the following:
1. Interview four or five people, Christians or non-Christians, asking them for their definition of teaching. Perhaps you'll want to use a cassette recorder. The point is to illustrate what teaching and learning mean in the framework of our culture. Bring these definitions to class, and discuss together any contrasts you discover between our culture's

notion of teaching and that which you see in Paul's letters.

2. Another approach is to ask some Sunday school teachers to state the goal of their teaching. You could avoid slanting the responses by interviewing children's teachers on Sunday morning, asking specifically, "What is your teaching goal for this morning?" Then discuss the taped answers with your class. What do these answers imply about Christian communication? How might Paul respond to these answers? Do you think they are like or unlike the goal of those who taught you when you were young?

INPUT

There are several ways of reviewing content while utilizing student participation.

Select one or more of the following:

1. If you assigned your class *personalize* 1 (pages 28-29), call on them at this time for reports. What did they discover about the nature of teaching and learning in their studies? As they share their definitions, have your students refer to the passages from which they drew their information.

2. List on the chalkboard the 1) subject matter and 2) methods of teaching Paul urges in 2 Timothy. Encourage class members to discuss each item as they find them.

3. You may wish to broaden the understanding of biblical teaching. You will find additional research material in the author's textbook, *A Theology of Christian Education* (Zondervan).

IMPACT

Select one or more of the following:

1. Place on the chalkboard Paul's statement from 1 Timothy 1:5: "The goal of this command is love, which comes from a pure heart, a good conscience and a sincere faith." Ask your students to share one thing that has helped them grow as Christians in love, purity, good conscience, and/or sincerity of faith. Note the circumstances briefly on the chalkboard and then analyze: In each case, what was it that God used to teach your students?

2. Or discuss *personalize* 2 on page 29.

3. Have the class design a Christian education program for third-graders. If we understand teaching in the Pauline sense of communicating both truth and life-style, what might be important elements of our nurture of third-graders? Who will be the teachers? What will be the teaching settings? What helps will we want to utilize?

ASSIGNMENT: Text chapter 3; selected *Going Deeper* items.

3
1, 2 Timothy; Titus

RELIABLE MEN

THIS SESSION FOCUSES on the unique role of spiritual leaders in teaching the church. It further clarifies the New Testament system of communicating faith by both verbal instruction and example. Because both truth and life-style must be communicated, it is important to select appropriate leaders.

One of two applications may be more significant for your class. You may want to help your students think through leadership qualifications for their own church.

LAUNCHING

Select one or more of the following:

1. Place on the chalkboard the following statement: "Only a person who lives the Christian life can guide others to a Christian life-style". As your students come in, ask them to talk with one other per-

son about the implications of this statement. Then discuss together the implications your students see. Their response will help you evaluate how clearly they have understood the concepts introduced in the chapter.

2. Or, place on the chalkboard lists from page 36 and ask your students to point out relationships between the two. Ask them to explain specifically why only a person like the one on the right can communicate a life-style like that described on the left.

3. Ask your students to evaluate the following phone conversation between members of the pulpit committee of a local church.

"Yes, yes, George, I know he's the more experienced man, but did you see the recommendations given young Whitworth? His professors say he's one of the most outstanding students they've had at the seminary. And you know how good his candidate sermon was. . . . No, I didn't know he was having trouble getting along with his parents, but after all, young people these days just naturally go through a period of rebellion. He'll come out of that as he matures. . . . The thing I'm thinking about is the future of this church. We've got to have a speaker who can attract folks. After all, we've got a big budget to meet, payments on the buildings are not getting any smaller, and unless we get a real good preacher I think we're in trouble. . . . No, there's no question about it, young Whitworth is the man for this church; and I, for one, am going to vote for him at our next committee meeting."

BIBLE ALIVE SERIES

INPUT

Select one or more of the following:

1. Turn to the list of qualifications for church leaders in either 1 Timothy or Titus. Ask your class to come up with either synonymous terms or with illustrations of how each quality might express itself today. The result should be a description of an individual qualified to be a spiritual leader and teacher of the congregation.

2. Examine in 1 and 2 Timothy every passage in which Paul refers to Timothy's intimate acquaintance with his teaching and way of life, or in which Paul encourages Timothy to pay attention to his teaching and his way of life. Read and discuss these passages together. What must leaders do if they wish to communicate their faith by example as well as by verbal instruction?

IMPACT

Ask class members to take the role of a theological "Ann Landers" who receives a number of inquiries from different church members. Divide your students into groups based on the question they choose to work on.

1. Dear Dr. Paul: I am a new Christian. I wonder how I can teach my children. I don't really know much but I want them to grow up to be good Christians.

2. Dear Dr. Paul: As president of our denominational seminary, I've been concerned that we de-

velop a program for equipping outstanding spiritual leaders for our churches. What do you think we should do to work toward this goal?

3. Dear Dr. Paul: I've just been chosen as an elder of our congregation. I really don't know what I ought to be doing. What is my task?

4. Dear Dr. Paul: We are going to be electing leaders in our church next week. What can I do to be sure that the right individuals are chosen?

5. Dear Dr. Paul: Some folks have been suggesting that anyone who is called as pastor of the church ought to be at least thirty-five years old. What do you think of this idea?

6. Dear Dr. Paul: As Sunday school superintendent, I wonder whether we ought to start sort of a Bible institute for our people with elective classes, or whether we ought to have adult class groups divided by age. What do you think would be the best approach? I'm concerned that our folks get some real solid Christian teaching.

Give each group a chance to answer their question. Then after each group reports, let the rest of the class discuss the problems and solutions.

ASSIGNMENT: Text chapter 4; selected *Going Deeper* items.

4
1, 2 Timothy; Titus

THE UNDERSHEPHERDS

IN THIS LESSON you might focus either on the nature and structure of leadership or on the question of the role of women in the church. Feel free to choose the most appropriate emphasis for your own group. Neither of these issues are academic: each has significance for the church and our age.

LAUNCHING

Select one or more of the following:
1. Read the quote from *probe* 1 (p. 52) to your class and ask for reactions. Response from your students should give you insight into their questions and needs.
2. Or, ask the women to respond to *personalize* 3 (p. 51). How do they feel as women in your church? Do they feel accepted and valued as persons? If not, why not? How is either acceptance or nonacceptance communicated to them by the congregation?

During this time it would be good to place the women in a circle facing each other and the men seated behind them in an outer circle. Do not let any of the men make comments while women discuss the question.

If you choose this approach, it will be helpful to then reverse the positions. Have the women seated in the outer circle and the men in the inside, discussing *personalize* 4. Do the men feel accepted and valued as persons or not? How do they communicate either acceptance or nonacceptance? How do they communicate acceptance or nonacceptance to women in the church?

INPUT

Select one or more of the following:

1. Ask each member of your class to prepare five quiz questions covering the content of this chapter. Divide the class into two teams and have a quiz-down. This is a simple and yet fun approach to review content.

2. Or, if you choose to focus on church leadership, ask your pastor or one of the church leaders to share for five to ten minutes his understanding of his role as a leader. Open the class for questions and interchange between the guest speaker and the students.

3. Or, if your focus is on women in the church, ask two women who hold different views on the question of leadership roles for women to prepare five-minute presentations explaining their points of view. Afterwards, open the class for discussion. En-

BIBLE ALIVE SERIES

courage the students to work from the biblical data in exploring issues with those who give the reports.

IMPACT

Select one or more of the following:

1. The author suggests that seeking fulfillment and being a whole person rather than seeking to be something one is not is the key to finding oneself in any situation. Does this help a woman who feels that she has not been given her full recognition and acceptance as a person?

2. Or, discuss how in the local church women can feel that they are of value in the congregation.

3. Or, work together as a class to draw a church organizational chart. Every organization should show not only the role of team leadership but also the critical aspect of communicating the faith. After your chart has been organized, talk about the practical implications of your structure.

Each of the topics for today are of serious import for the church and will not be resolved in a single class hour. But do pray that today's study may help clarify some of the issues and give future guidance to members of your class and congregation.

ASSIGNMENT: Text chapter 5; selected *Going Deeper* items.

5
Jude; 2 Peter

TIMES OF STRESS

THIS SESSION INTRODUCES the subject of heresy and apostasy. Your goal is not to recreate the Inquisition but to help members of your class recognize dangers that can arise from within the church, and to know what response the Christian can make. In preparation for this session, your students have surveyed 2 Peter and Jude. You will probably want to adopt a survey or summary approach for this class, getting into details in greater depth during your next meeting, which continues this study of the warnings to the church.

LAUNCHING

Select one or more of the following:

1. You might want to begin class by listing key terms, such as *epithumia* and *nous*, on the chalkboard. Ask your students to jot down brief definitions of the two. Then discuss the definitions.

2. Ask, "Have you ever known a false teacher in a church you've attended?" Encourage open discussion and sharing for a few minutes before moving into the study itself.

3. Or, put this statement on the chalkboard and ask your students to respond to it: *A person who believes wrong doctrine is not necessarily a false teacher.*

4. Your students may bring out the point that some Christians may have a lack of understanding or may have had incorrect teaching that would lead to erroneous beliefs. Sometimes it may be difficult to tell whether a lack of growth or a commitment to untruth is at the root of disagreements. If your students want to think about how they might respond to these different situations, give them time for such an exploration.

INPUT

Select one or more of the following:

1. Divide the class into groups. Ask each to locate three passages that focus on the life-style of false teachers. When this brief research has been concluded, have the groups come together and report and discuss their findings.

2. Or ask those who explored one of the topics under *personalize* 1 on page 64 to report.

In each of these approaches your goal is to encourage your students to summarize and pinpoint specific teachings on the subject of false teachers that they have discovered in their study of Jude and 2 Peter.

IMPACT

Select one or more of the following:

1. The subject of false teachers is given careful consideration in the New Testament. We need to be able to recognize them; we need to understand their motives and the approach they take as they seek to draw others away from the truth. We need to know how to respond to these teachers and how to keep ourselves pure.

In the next lesson you will look at these areas more intensively. For now, your goal is to open a discussion that will not necessarily resolve all the questions but will begin to explore some of the complexities of this issue. One discussion starter is to have your students label a series of statements true or false. Then discuss and give reasons for the answers they gave. The goal of this exercise is not to decide the rightness or wrongness of each point; there is no absolutely correct answer for the following items.

A false teacher should be immediately exposed and driven out of the church.

You can only tell a false teacher when he denies the deity of Christ.

A false teacher will never influence a true Christian.

Feeling strong sexual desires is the first step toward apostasy.

Bitterness, competitiveness, and pride are traits in leaders that make us suspect they are false teachers.

It is not so important that we understand our faith as it is that we live a good and holy life.

It is so important to keep the church doctrinally pure that it's all right if we mistakenly attack a few young Christians. It's a price well worth paying.

Your students may feel a little upset about being asked for specific answers to these questions. Encourage them to go back into Scripture and to settle the doubts that may have been raised. Reassure them that the next class meeting will continue to explore this very important area.

ASSIGNMENT: Text chapter 6; selected *Going Deeper* items.

6

Jude; 2 Peter

HERESY!

IN THIS STUDY your group will look at the biblical definition of heresy. The particular stress of the lesson should be on how to respond to heresy in the church and how to protect oneself against its dangers. Your goal is for your students to have a fresh sense of confidence in their own personal relationship with God. They also need a clear awareness of how to respond in a situation in which the integrity of their faith is attacked.

LAUNCHING

Select one or more of the following:

1. You might begin with a quiz asking the four items listed under *personalize* 2 on page 76. After each person has jotted down one answer in each of the four areas, share the responses given.

BIBLE ALIVE SERIES

2. On the chalkboard place the following equation for your class to discuss: *heresy = deviousness.* To what extent is this an accurate representation of the biblical meaning of heresy? To what extent is it inadequate? What kind of a definition of heresy can you and your class work out?

INPUT

Select one or more of the following:

Your students may be thoroughly familiar with the content of 2 Peter and Jude by this time. If so, you may wish to move toward the application activities under *Impact* below. If you feel there is still confusion concerning some of the teachings of these books, use some of the following.

1. In groups of four, have your students quickly move through these two epistles. Half the groups should locate verses that describe the approach or appeal of false teachers and the content of their teaching. The other half of the groups should seek to pinpoint recognizable characteristics of false teachers. After ten minutes of study, have the groups share their reports.

2. Or trace the argument of 2 Peter 1 and 3 by reading the chapters aloud paragraph by paragraph as it relates to Peter's theme of warning against false teachers. This is the approach in the text, pages 73-76. This exercise will enable your students to express themselves in their own words and will help crystalize their understanding of this important teaching.

IMPACT

Select one or more of the following:

1. List on the board the three principles to guide our response when we confront false teaching (pp. 71-72). Ask your students to explain the principles and then come up with one or more illustrations of how each would operate in a specific situation.

2. How might the first readers of Jude's doxology have felt, and why? What kind of confidence does it give us, in spite of dangers that exist from within the church?

3. Give a mini-lecture, summarizing the protection we have today against false teachers (pp. 73-75). Help your students feel a deepening sense of confidence in their own personal relationships with Jesus Christ. Encourage them to the disciplines of the Christian life Peter describes that will lead each to stability and maturity.

ASSIGNMENT: Text chapter 7; selected *Going Deeper* items.

7

1 John 1:1–2:2

THE DISCIPLE JESUS LOVED

IN THIS SESSION you will briefly discuss John's character and then focus on his reason for writing the major teachings of 1 John 1. We are moving into the deeply personal section of our "last word" letter studies. Pray that as you teach these lessons, special needs of your students will be met.

LAUNCHING

Select one or more of the following:
1. Place on the chalkboard a chart representing John's character. At the left end jot down the characteristics revealed in John's early life (p. 82). On the far right indicate some of the qualities John has developed by the time he writes these letters (p. 83). After talking about his personality growth and transformation, ask your students to draw a line representing themselves. On the left they should jot down characteristics of their personalities at their

conversion or at a selected point in the past. On the far right have them write down the qualities they want to see fully developed in their own personalities. Have each one put a check mark along the line to indicate his or her position at the moment. Then break into groups of three or four to share what is currently helping or hindering each person on that journey.

2. The author suggests that fellowship indicates a comfortable relationship with God. Have your students discuss this concept. Encourage them to share what has in the past or present led them to feel uncomfortable in their relationship with Him. Record these answers on the chalkboard.

3. Or, give a mini-lecture giving historical background on John the Apostle. Focus on the fact that John's transformation holds out hope for each one of us. Be sure also to point out that he was a disciple whom Jesus loved even in his very immature days. Our present lack of growth does not interrupt God's full commitment and love to us.

INPUT

Select one or more of the following:

1. John uses words in a very distinctive and theological way. Important words in this first chapter include *light, darkness, life, and truth.* You may wish to take time to do a personal study or to assign research projects and reports to some of your students. If so, give three to five minutes to each term so that your students are clear about its meaning.

2. Or you may wish to focus on the very important discussion on walking in the light. Sometimes a way of clarifying a passage like this is to think it through verse by verse with your students. Then have pairs of students write down two things that walking in the light does not mean, and two things that this teaching does mean. Then, list the findings on the chalkboard.

You may want to explain that the Greek word for "confess" does not mean "to say you are sorry and promise to never do it again." Instead it is to look at an action and to agree with God that His perception of the act as sin is correct. This kind of acknowledgement to God and honesty with Him is critical if we are to experience His forgiveness and cleansing.

When you are sure that your students understand the essential teaching of this important Bible passage, move onto the application activities.

IMPACT

Select one or more of the following:

1. Discuss in teams or as a class the individuals described in *personalize* 3 (page 91). What need is the individual most likely to have? How can the teaching of 1 John 1 meet that need?

2. You might close by having sentence prayers, in which each student can thank God for ways in which this chapter meets his or her needs.

ASSIGNMENT: Text chapter 8; selected *Going Deeper* items.

8
1 John 2:3–3:10

TO KNOW HIM

IN HARMONY with the thrust of John's first letter, this study also focuses on a question of personal relationship. Specifically the question John deals with is, "How can we be sure we know Him?" It is important to understand that the cause of the doubts with which John is concerned in this section of this book is the individual's failure to live the kind of life he knows God wants for him. It's not uncommon for a believer to doubt his own relationship with God if he has been a Christian for a length of time and is troubled by failures and temptations. To all of us who have such doubts, John brings encouraging insights.

LAUNCHING

Select one or more of the following:
  1. Put this simple true/false quiz on the board:
  Obedience is God's way for us to test others' relationship to Him.

A desire to respond to Christ and a growing love for others is a basis for confidence that we know Jesus.

We must live a sinless life after our conversion or we have not really been saved.

The pattern of the believer's life rather than specific actions will demonstrate to others his personal relationship to God.

It is possible for us as Christians not to sin.

After everyone has had a chance to write down the answers, let the class discuss the questions. Your goal is to give an opportunity for individuals to demonstrate their understanding of the principles taught in this chapter and let you see areas that need to be clarified.

2. Or, ask your students, seated in a circle, to share about times when they have had uncertainty about their relationship with God. Encourage two or three to talk about their feelings and to share anything that may have helped give them confidence in that relationship.

3. Another possibility is to list on the chalkboard 1 John 3:9, "No one who is born of God will continue to sin." Ask your class to brainstorm with you as to how this verse should be understood. How might this verse be understood if it were taken out of its 1 John context and seen as a threat, a warning, or as an attempt to shame? How might we feel if we heard these words addressed to us by God and saw each of these different motives underlying the statement? What evidence do we have in 1 John that the tone of voice is one of promise? What personal application can we make of this promise?

INPUT

Select one or more of the following:

1. You might want to survey the concept of internal evidence of relationship, as developed in this chapter. As we mature in our faith, we find ourselves more obedient. And even a new Christian can feel a deep desire to respond to Jesus and take the first faltering steps of obedience.

2. *Personalize* 4 asks your students to find fifteen statements about sin in 1 John 2:28—3:10. List these on the chalkboard as the class suggests them. Ask the students to explain each statement and illustrate it from 1 John.

3. Another option is to do a brief study on the Bible's teaching about the Holy Spirit as teacher. Some research on your part should provide a very exciting mini-lecture and should increase your students' confidence that as they study they can understand the Word of God without an authoritative teacher present to interpret each statement.

IMPACT

Select one or more of the following:

1. You might tape a counseling situation as imagined by one or more of your students (see *personalize* 5). Play the counselee's explanation of the problem and then in groups of two or three discuss how 1 John might minister to this particular need.

2. Ask your class to imagine a church board meeting. A member of the church expresses a desire to

start a Bible study group in his home. This individual's idea is that the group would not have any designated teacher, but each person would study a common passage of Scripture during the week and then share what God had been showing him/her in connection with that passage. The group would then pray and help each other to apply the teachings that had been revealed.

What might be possible reactions from members of the church board? What are the arguments against this leaderless approach to Bible study? What might be some positive values? How does the fact that the Holy Spirit is the teacher help us resolve such practical questions in the church?

Close by briefly summarizing the inner evidences available to us of a real and vital relationship with God. How good it is to be aware that He wants to be sure we know Him.

ASSIGNMENT: Text chapter 9; selected *Going Deeper* items.

9

1 John 3:11–4:21

CALLED TO LOVE

RESPONDING IN LOVE to our brothers is so deeply embedded in the nature of Christian experience that it in itself becomes an objective test of our relationship with God. We know we know Him, John says, when we love one another. God is love, and he who walks in love lives in God.

LAUNCHING

Select one or both of the following:

1. To focus on love, you might place a simple chart on the chalkboard. On one side write the name *Cain* and on the other side write the name *Christ*. Ask the class members to develop as many contrasts between the two as possible. Then list the ways in which Christ expressed His love.

Point out particularly that both love and hate must find expression in behavior.

2. You might begin with reports on *personalize* 1, in

which your students underlined the most significant statement, the most puzzling statement, and the most helpful statement in this section of 1 John. Working in small groups or in a larger circle, have individuals share one of the three items they selected.

INPUT

Select one or both of the following:

1. Review the chart on page 108. It points out that there are objective as well as inner evidences of love. Be sure students understand this emphasis of 1 John.

2. Or trace the thought of 1 John 4: 7-21. John describes the nature of love and its expression in the community of believers. Remember that this is not something we are responsible to create in our own hearts. This is God's statement of what will be produced in those who have a deep relationship with Him.

IMPACT

Select one or more of the following:

1. Stan's story (pp. 112-113) gives a good illustration of how the kind of love John talks about encourages transformation. Read through the story together. Have your students known anyone who has had a similar experience? Do they know anyone who may need this kind of love?

2. Another possible focus for application is the

teaching that "perfect love drives out fear" (1 John 4:18). In John's day, there were some whose hearts condemned them. They did not feel free and cared for in their own personal relationship with God. The awareness that we are loved drives out that fear. A vital element in bringing us the certainty of Christ's love is to experience it through others.

3. Focus on expressions of love within your own church family. How is love presently being expressed? How is it being felt by members of your class? Work together on the theme introduced by *personalize* 3 (p. 114). What specifically can your students do to take more initiative in showing love to each other?

ASSIGNMENT: Text chapter 10; selected *Going Deeper* items.

10

1 John 5; 2, 3 John

ETERNAL LIFE

THIS IS AN IMPORTANT CHAPTER and yet is one containing several problem passages, the meaning of which have been subjects of much debate. You may find it helpful to assign research on these various passages and hear reports in class. Or you may simply want to accept the suggested explanation in the textbook and focus your attention upon the nature of faith as it relates to eternal life.

One particularly relevant activity would be to go through 2 and 3 John with your students and pick up themes from 1 John that explain or give added dimension to the later letters.

LAUNCHING

Select one or more of the following:

   1. On the chalkboard write, "Faith in Jesus is like ..." Ask your students either to draw a picture demonstrating the nature of Christian faith as they

understand it, or to complete the sentence with a phrase. For instance, someone might say, "Faith in Jesus is like putting your hand in the hand of someone who you know will never let you down."

2. Or, ask each of your students to express in a single sentence what eternal life means to him or her. This will build on *personalize* 2 (p. 124).

3. Select some of the key words found in the Gospel of John and ask each of your students to select one that has the greatest personal meaning to him or her. Appropriate key words could include the following: *truth, life, light, love, eternal life.*

INPUT

Select one or both of the following:

1. You may find it appropriate to spend a few minutes on some of the three problem passages identified in the text. However, talking about speculative issues should never become the focus of any class. You should spend time here if a personal concern is expressed by any of your students. You might simply ask if any of these issues or areas really trouble any of your students. If not, move on.

2. An excellent way to review all the teachings of 1 John is to go through either 2 or 3 John with your students. As you read the letter verse by verse, discuss what teachings in 1 John make it clear the apostle's concerns. Ask for a personal interpretation of the verses that can be related to 1 John. This could be an exciting and possibly extended activity for your students. It will help them grasp how much

they have learned in the four weeks of studying John's letters.

IMPACT

Select one or both of the following:

1. It may very well be that working through 2 or 3 John will provide opportunity for application as well as take a large block of class time. If so, do not worry about an *Impact* activity. Conclude with prayer, asking several to express to God thanks for particular truths that have been meaningful to them.

2. Or, you may wish to use the learning activity suggested for *Launching* 3.

ASSIGNMENT: Text chapter 11; selected *Going Deeper* items. It would be appropriate next week to spend perhaps half of your class time on a review of the concepts taught in the "last word" letters. You might ask your students to develop four or five review questions they would like to see on a test should there be one. Do not plan for a test, but use their suggested review questions as a basis for discussion.

11
selected New Testament passages

GOD'S PERSONAL TOUCH

THE LAST THREE CHAPTERS in this book summarize distinctive contributions of the New Testament. These summaries draw together a number of significant themes emphasized in the earlier **Bible Alive** New Testament studies.

A special teaching format is suggested for each of these chapters. This format involves a weekly discussion and sharing time that will place greater emphasis on your students' personal discoveries. The teaching suggestions focus on ways to initiate and guide this discussion.

In this particular session, a more specific review of the preceding ten chapters of this book is suggested. You can, of course, choose whether or not to include the review feature.

REVIEW

1. Place on the chalkboard the following review

chart to summarize the major contributions of each of the Scripture passages we've explored. On the board, make a third column with the heading "TEST QUESTIONS AND ANSWERS" (see assignment, chapter 10; review questions).

PASSAGES	KEY TEACHINGS
Pastoral Epistles (1, 2 Timothy; Titus)	The nature of teaching The qualification of leaders The role of leaders
Jude; 2 Peter	Characteristics of false teaching, false teachers Response to false teaching, false teachers
1 John 1	Walking in light
1 John 2:1—3:10	Inner evidence of relationship with God
1 John 3:11—4:21	Outer evidence of relationship with God
1 John 5; 2, 3 John	Eternal life

Work through the chart section by section, asking your students to share questions relating to that section that they generated for last week's quiz questions assignment. Working through the chart and asking and answering students' questions should provide a meaningful review of the themes and significance of the "last word" epistles.

DISCUSSION

Let your students become panels of experts on the topics outlined in chapter 11. You'll recall that each student was to study intensively one of the topics and

to read the key Bible passages of at least two of the topics. Simply talk through each topic in order, letting those students who focused on a particular topic be the authorities. The information you want from the experts would include such insights as:
- What seems to be the most significant teaching?
- What do you think is the personal meaning of this truth for believers today?
- How important is this teaching to Christians?

ASSIGNMENT: Text chapter 12; selected *Going Deeper* items.

12

selected New Testament passages

GOD STOOPS TO CARE

IN THIS CHAPTER your focus is on the personal God as He is revealed in the New Testament. It's exciting to sense the completeness of His love for and commitment to us.

DISCUSSION

Read aloud Psalm 89:24-27. Ask several of your students to pick one thought or phrase from these verses that tells them something exciting about the person of God.

Then ask your students to share what they discovered from the key passages about God that gave them a new awareness of Him. With about ten minutes left in the class, distribute paper and crayons. Ask your students to draw pictures symbolizing their perceptions of God. They can use colors and shapes to portray His person and attitudes or their sense of relationship with Him. Have each student

PASS IT ON

explain his or her picture to at least one other individual in the class.

ASSIGNMENT: Text chapter 13; selected *Going Deeper* items.

13

selected passages

GOD AND HIS FAMILY

YOU WILL WANT TO USE a discussion format for the final study of your session. Share how vital it is to reaffirm the family relation we have with other believers and to find ways to build that relationship with one another. Your discussion should focus on the positive rather than on any negative dimensions.

DISCUSSION

You and your class should be sitting in a circle so each can see the others. You might begin by reminding the students that you have been working together as members of God's family. During this time, God has been ministering through each to others. Suggest that class members express their appreciation to others for any contributions they've made to their lives. You might begin by speaking directly to one of the students, saying something like: "Jay, I particularly appreciate your responsiveness. You've made me feel very comfortable and appreciated," or something similar. Individuals should speak directly to another member of the class and simply say thanks and mention what he or she appreciates about the other person.

After this sharing time, which can take as much of the class hour as necessary, ask your students what they learned concerning life in God's family. Encourage discussion based on the sharing.

In concluding your time together, you may want to review the idea that the Incarnation continues in and through the church. Christ still walks the earth in members of His body and through us shares Himself with our brothers and sisters as well as with those who do not yet know Jesus in a personal way.

You may also find some of your students want to discuss *personalize* 5. Be guided by the interests and concerns of your men and women.

It would be very appropriate to close by linking hands and singing a song such as "Believer in the Family," or "We are One in the Spirit."

If you are using a final examination, schedule it for some other time than during this final class hour.

One final **Bible Alive** New Testament survey textbook, *His Glory,* focuses on the person of Christ as He is revealed in the Gospel of John and Revelation.